The Creative
WATER GARDENER

The Creative
WATER GARDENER

ANDREW WILSON

WARD LOCK

For Rebecca and Naomi

A WARD LOCK BOOK

First published in the UK 1995
by Ward Lock
Wellington House
125 Strand
LONDON
WC2R 0BB

A Cassell Imprint

First paperback edition 1996

Distributed in the United States
by Sterling Publishing Co., Inc.
387 Park Avenue South, New York, NY 10016-8810

Distributed in Australia
by Capricorn Link (Australia) Pty Ltd
2/13 Carrington Road, Castle Hill NSW 2154

A British Library Cataloguing in Publication Data block for this book may be
obtained from the British Library

ISBN 0-7063-7478-9
Typeset by Litho Link Ltd, Welshpool, Powys, United Kingdom
Printed and bound in Spain

Cover photographs: Front inset and back image courtesy of Clive Nichols.
Front main image Andrew Lawson, Ash Tree Cottage, Kilmington, Wilts.

CONTENTS

ACKNOWLEDGEMENTS

Special thanks should go to Kris Laws of LWL Landscapes who provided a great deal of technical and general background information to make this book possible. His help in this project has been invaluable.

Additionally I should thank John Brookes, Isabelle Green and Anthony Paul for their submissions in Chapter 1, Chris Thornton of Outdoor Lighting Supplies for his help with Chapter 8 and Peter Thurman for his help with Chapter 9.

Photographs are by Roger Foley: p. 117; The Garden Picture Library: pp. 22, 72 (left); Jerry Harpur: pp. 19, 26, 38, 96; Andrew Lawson: pp. 36, 60, 94; Clive Nichols: pp. 13, 15, 24, 31, 32, 52, 56, 63, 75 and front cover inset (Designer: Anthony Noel), 84, 86 (Japanese Garden, Chelsea 1993. Woking Borough Council), 87, 88 and back cover, 92, 95, 112, 113, 120; Outdoor Lighting Supplies: pp. 98, 102; Hugh Palmer: 8, 16, 58, 81; Wildlife Matters: pp. 18, 21, 34, 108, 111.

PREFACE

W ater in the landscape never fails to attract us. It is one of the four basic elements, and it teems with life, movement and drama, changing in character with every atmospheric nuance. It comes as no surprise, therefore, that water should also prove popular within the garden. Here, when we seek solace or refreshment, water provides these qualities in abundance.

The inspiration for the use of water in garden design comes either from the natural landscapes we have seen or from a more abstract symbolism, perhaps associated with religion or belief. However, the successful translation of water in the landscape, or water as a spiritual symbol, into water in the garden is a most difficult task. In the first place there is often a remarkable difference in scale; then, the imitation of nature may be restricted by circumstance, or the specific religious connotations may be lost on a civilization with different values.

These difficulties do not and should not prevent us from experimenting with and introducing water into our gardens as a source of pleasure and excitement. The following chapters aim to assist in these endeavours, first by setting creative and inventive ideas in an historical context and then by considering the individual elements that are associated with water, from jets and spouts to lighting and planting. The suggestions aim to encompass as many different garden applications as possible, supported by practical design considerations that will enable the reader to introduce water successfully into the smallest balcony garden or the largest estate.

The purpose of this book is to show creative and exciting responses to the use of water within the garden and to inspire or animate our approach to this most mesmerizing of elements.

chapter one

The
HISTORICAL CONTEXT

W ater is essential to our existence, and it has been praised, valued, esteemed and revered since humans first cultivated the earth in early history. Because water supported crops and fruits that could be harvested to provide essential food, it came to symbolize life itself. It is not difficult to understand, therefore, how water came to play such a central role in many of the world's religions. Water purifies, rejuvenates and supports all forms of life, and without this basic element nothing would exist.

The first garden, the Old Testament tells us, was located to the north of Babylon, created by God for mankind, supposedly in the image of heaven:

> In the day that the Lord God made the earth and the heavens, when no plant of the field was yet in the earth and no herb of the field had yet sprung up – for the Lord God had not caused it to rain upon the earth and there was no man to till the ground; but a mist went up from the earth and watered the whole face of the ground – then the Lord God formed man of the dust
>
> And the Lord God planted a garden in Eden, in the east; and there he put the man whom he had formed.
>
> A river flowed out of Eden to water the garden . . . (and) . . . the Lord God took the man and put him in the garden to till it and keep it.
>
> Genesis, Chapter 2

The dramatic use of water in the sun-drenched courtyard gardens of Granada's Generalife illustrates the importance of this element in the Islamic garden. The strong geometric layout is also typical.

The civilizations that developed around Mesopotamia shared the themes outlined in Genesis as part of their religions. The Garden of Eden as described in the Bible was watered by a river that divided into four, the Pishon, the Gihon, the Tigris and the Euphrates. In Persian, Byzantine and Islamic cultures the idea of a garden fed by four rivers and forming some kind of paradise on earth is common, and similar themes may be traced through the symbolic art of Buddhism.

The number four is basic to these themes, and the four rivers came to be represented in many gardens by irrigation channels. Often the world would be shown divided into four sections with a centrally located spring. The early gardens also used the square or rectangle to identify an overall shape. The *charah bagh* was created, a quadripartite garden, which became a standard design concept for centuries.

WATER IN THE GARDENS OF ISLAM

Muhammed founded Islam in the seventh century AD, and, as with many other religions, the idea of a paradise or heaven was a central concept. The Koran refers to a paradise garden, furnished with cool shade, fruits and fountains of running water, which represents the reward for true believers.

The art of garden design was important in Islam, and the gardens that resulted from this culture were models of the heavenly paradise on earth. The gardens would be enclosed to allow for private meditation, geometric in their layout for symbolic and functional purposes and designed around water, the purifying and life-giving element that decorated and cooled the warm atmosphere. Canals or channels of some description typically divided the garden into four distinct sections. Water, in the form of a square or rectangular pool, was often also used as a central focus. In some gardens the very centre might have been occupied by a pavilion, with water channels converging on, or flowing around, the structure. The pavilion provided a platform for panoramic views into and around the garden. The other important view was from the main entrance gateway, usually highly ornamented, into the garden towards the pavilion. In smaller gardens, because of the restrictions of scale, the pool was the most important feature.

The water and pathway systems were fiercely geometric, which resulted in axial and symmetrical rectilinear patterns. The planting fell into two categories – flowering plants for colour or scent and trees for shade and fruit. The vegetation softened the strong geometry and decorated the straight, man-made shapes. The pathways leading to or from the pavilion or the central water feature were further decorated by smaller structures or gateways, which reinforced the axial design. Generally, a flat site was chosen, but the spread of Islam caused sloping ground to be used to good effect in the creation of terraces with water cascades and fountains.

Perhaps the idea of the oasis was the natural predecessor of these gardens, but in the hot climates of the Mediterranean and western Asia water lay at the very heart of civilization. Of the elements used in the design of the Islamic garden water was the most decorative and certainly the most sacred. Moving water was used to excite the senses, fountains were carved or decorated to amplify the spectacle, and at night candles or lamps were floated on the surface of the water to create a tranquil but celestial effect.

These gardens were created throughout the Islamic world. The Moors introduced the art of garden design to the West and, in the famous gardens of the Alhambra and Generalife near Granada, illustrated the principles of geometric layout and the importance of water. In the enclosed courtyards and terraces of these two gardens fountains, water staircases, canals and simple pools typify the decorative use of water.

In the East the Islamic influence mixed with the traditions of India to create spectacular gardens with water cascades, channels and basins. In the Kashmir region, where water was plentiful, the Mogul emperors created splendid paradise gardens, matched only for beauty by the surrounding landscape. Gravity-fed fountains created lively displays, canals of water linked different parts of the gardens, and at night cascades were lit from behind to provide glowing streams of sound and activity. These features are illustrated by the Shalamar Bagh on the shores of Lake Dal, where a series of terraces laid out on the quadripartite system based on irrigation channels can also be seen.

In between these two extremes, the gardens of Iran, Turkey, Afghanistan and north Africa show the wide variety of design that is possible from these basic elements.

WATER IN THE GARDENS OF CHINA

In spite of all the stylistic developments in the art of garden design elsewhere in the world, China has remained a bastion of conservatism, with a continuous thread of philosophical influence stretching back for thousands of years.

One of the main Chinese philosophies, Daoism, developed the idea that human beings are an harmonious part of nature and the gardens of China came to reflect this belief. Landscape was developed and improved by human artifice, and water was used within this framework to create meandering streams, dramatic waterfalls or tranquil pools designed to reflect the moon.

The rigid geometry of the paradise garden would not have found favour in the Chinese garden, where the imititation of nature lead to softer shapes particularly with reference to water. Ironically, the interior of Chinese homes would have been formally and geometrically designed, and against this framework the garden would work as a strong contrast.

Chinese gardens were related to the experience of landscape painting. Views or vistas were carefully controlled so that the story of the garden unfolded with a progression through a series of tableaux. Water and rocks created the basic framework into which buildings and garden structures were placed or hidden and the planting was carefully selected to decorate and soften the forms.

The rocks were built up to form the equivalent of contemporary rockeries, solid, hard and masculine (yang). The harmony necessary in the garden was provided by the water, soft, tranquil and feminine (yin). Water provided the largest flat surface, forming the focal point in most gardens. Retained by rocks and stones, the mirror-like surface of the water was designed for quiet contemplation, reflected patterns and harmony.

WATER IN THE GARDENS OF JAPAN

Garden design in Japan has been subject to many influences. Historically, Chinese culture was strong, but the later important philosophies of Buddhism and Shinto introduced strong religious symbolism into the garden, together with a need for ceremonial activity. Water continued to be a strong feature or an important consideration in garden design.

During the Heian period, between the eighth and twelfth centuries, the Chinese influence was strong, and lakes or reflective pools were common, some large enough to take boats for sailing parties. Later, through the influence of Zen Buddhism, dry gardens became an important aspect of garden design. Water was suggested by raked gravel or by arrangements of stones to imitate, in an abstract sense, the movement or presence of water.

In the Momoyama period the tea ceremony, which was accompanied by rituals using water for purification and cleansing, became central to the design of gardens in Japan. The *tsukubai* or stone water basin, a large stone or boulder with a carved or shaped basin filled with water, was used for these rituals. The basins are now traditional features used more for decoration than for ceremony.

In the contemporary Japanese garden water is used in still, reflective pools or to provide movement in flowing streams or waterfalls that imitate the natural landscape. In a similar way to the Chinese idea, however, the fluidity of water is also used as a contrast to the solid mass of stone.

Both the Chinese and the Japanese styles have influenced European garden design to some extent, particularly during the eighteenth and nineteenth centuries, when the styles were taken up in reaction to the pervasive formal styles fashionable at the time.

WATER IN EUROPEAN GARDENS

Italy

In the garden designs of Europe water was often used more as a purely decorative device than as a symbolic or ritualistic element. In Italy, however, there is some evidence of a Moorish influence in the ancient gardens of the south, where colonnaded courtyards, channels and fountains in the tradition of Islam were built.

Towards the Renaissance the classical style was developed, and formal gardens on the grand and powerful scale became dominant. The use of water reached a climax at Villa d'Este, Tivoli with the pathway of a hundred fountains and various hydraulically operated beasts which populated the garden and amused visitors. Water channels, tiers and terraces form the central features of Villa Lante at Bagnaia, near Viterbo, and there are dramatic cascades at Villa Aldobrandini and Villa Torlonia, Frascati. Here, the water was brought to the garden by means of an aqueduct, which fed a water theatre and other features.

The absence of decorative flowers in Italian gardens made water an important focal point and a strong contrast to the refined and elegant greenery and geometry of the formal style.

France

The formal style was also typical of French garden design, and Versailles was the ultimate in regal splendour. In France, however, water was used in controlled shapes as part of the overall design or visual effect. The canal was widely used to provide a geometrically precise, reflective surface. Many of the larger châteaux were surrounded by moats, and the canal feature may have developed from this background.

The gardens of Versailles produced some of the most dramatic water features in terms of both design and engineering. Many of these ornate confections are still operational.

Later, designers developed more elaborate water patterns, with whole parterres of decorative pools creating a lively tapestry spread out before the principle rooms. Vaux-le-Vicomte, Seine-et-Marne, illustrates a dramatic use of water, which runs as a constant theme throughout the entire garden. André Le Nôtre (1613–1700) was responsible for the creation of this most imaginative garden, which represents his first great contribution to French garden design. With particular care he placed in the garden a rectangular pool, the Grand Miroir d'Eau, that once reached, provides a reflection of the entire façade of the château. He later used a similar theme for the Parterre d'Eau at Versailles.

Britain

Examples of formal water designs are evident in Britain, but the style did not last as on the Continent. Hampton Court, Greater London, has a most magnificent canal, the Long Water, which stretches out into the holm park. On a smaller scale the formal canal feature at Westbury Court, Gloucester, shows the Dutch influence, and Chatsworth House, Derbyshire, is famous for the great cascade, which drops water down a flight of shallow steps for some distance.

By the eighteenth century the landscape school had transformed garden design through the use of softer lines and irregular shapes. These features were no less grand and dramatic in scale, but the apparent sympathy with nature evident in this style found favour over the more obvious control of nature proposed by the formalists. Lancelot 'Capability' Brown (1716–83) regularly dammed and altered water courses to provide glimpses of meandering water in the distance or to provide stunning bridge crossings on the journey up to the house. Later, the irregular, curvilinear forms became prominent in public parks and pleasure gardens and spread worldwide.

WATER IN THE TWENTIETH-CENTURY GARDEN

The stylistic influences outlined so far are relevant to the design of water features within the garden, but the sheer scale of many of these features is difficult to comprehend and virtually impossible for most of us to imitate. However, many themes and concepts may be discerned in these historical references and translated into a more modern idiom.

In the development from Victorian to Edwardian style, the grand British garden reached a climax of extravagance and richness. The combination of inventive geometric layout provided by Edwin Lutyens (1869–1944), combined with the sensational colour-schemed planting of Gertrude Jekyll

The Water Terrace at Blenheim shows the influence of formality in the English garden, which was often swept aside by the landscape school.

(1843–1932), proved to be dramatic and memorable. Water often figured in their designs, which typified the Arts and Crafts Movement, revelling in pattern, shape and high quality workmanship.

Huge tanks of water for mirror-smooth reflections and narrow rills or canals featured regularly, often planted with marginal or aquatic plants. The gardens of Hestercombe near Taunton, Somerset, or the Deanery, Sonning, Berkshire, illustrate perfectly how water should be used to create atmosphere and excitement. Lutyens often played with water, creating storage systems or manipulating rainwater pipes, but the pools he introduced were mainly calm and still, with little consideration for fountains and jets. His design for the Mogul Gardens around the Viceroy's House at New Delhi has a curiously modern feel, an interesting meeting of styles with wide canals and a strong geometric layout.

Harold Peto (1828–97) followed Lutyens' example at Buscot Park, Faringdon, Oxfordshire, where an elegant flight of water steps drops down the slope from the house to the lake. The simplicity of the geometry, with its combination of rectangles and circles, is essential to the effect. The regular placing of water lilies planted in baskets gives a rhythm to the design that is most attractive, and the use of simple green hedging gives an Italian flavour to the design, a favourite theme of Peto's.

As the century progressed the face of design and of society changed dramatically. The suburbs expanded, and smaller, private gardens became customary and owners were keen to develop gardens of their own. The Modern Movement influenced garden design and provided excitement and the thrill of the new.

In Britain the style failed to make a lasting impression and designers and garden owners eventually reverted to the Edwardian dream gardens of herbaceous borders and gravel terraces.

Christopher Tunnard was one British landscape architect who did seize the initiative of the Modern Movement with the exciting results that may be seen in the gardens at Chertsey, Surrey, and Halland, Sussex. He later emigrated to the United States, leaving the Modern Movement in British garden design in a rather poor state.

British garden designers, such as Geoffrey Jellicoe, Sylvia Crowe and Russell Page, have experimented with this style, and their use of water in garden and landscape design is exciting and diverse. This approach may be unusual in Britain where, in general, garden design languishes in a pre-Modern malaise. The British tend to think of their gardens as homes for their plants for, as Sylvia Crowe said: 'One [attitude] is that the purpose of a garden is to grow plants, the other is that plants are one of the materials used in the creation of a garden'. However, across the world contemporary garden design has evolved dramatically and dynamically into an art form worthy of the twentieth century.

The water cascade at Buscot Park, designed by Harold Peto, is a masterpiece of elegant formality. The strong geometry and restricted range of materials create a strong impact.

In Mexico Luis Barragan works with basic abstract forms, sheets of water, walls of pure colour and simple planting to create atmosphere and a sense of power. These themes are evident in his design for the Plaza del Bebedero de los Caballos, Mexico City, where a centrally placed horse-trough brims over with reflective water and shadows from overhead tree canopies and trunks decorated with intricate patterns lie against colour washed walls.

In the United States Thomas Church produced a garden of breathtaking abstract beauty. On a hilltop overlooking the Sonoma valley, New Mexio, he created the El Novillero garden, which has a swimming pool as a centre piece. The swirling curves of the graceful but simple design reflect the shapes evident in the landscape of the valley below and beyond the perimeter of the garden.

These gardens are now important in historical terms, and contemporary style has moved on to accommodate their influence along with many others. Water is still an enduring element, sometimes symbolic, sometimes functional and sometimes purely decorative. Designers use water in many different ways, but their breadth of vision can provide a stimulus and an influence that affects our approach to the design of the water garden.

BELOW The inspired shaping of the El Novillero garden, designed by Thomas Church, relates directly to the landscape of the Sonoma Valley below, with its meandering ribbons of water.

ABOVE *The water garden at Denmans, designed by John Brookes. This still, reflective pool, surrounded by textured foliage plants and a cobble beach is ideal for quiet contemplation.*

Three prominent contemporary garden and landscape designers share their feelings for water below, describing how this element is utilized and included in their design work.

John Brookes, Sussex, UK

I am not a 'watery' sort of person, actually. I positively loathe trickly little streams of water prettied up with marginals in a domestic garden setting, called, I think, 'naturalistic'. Perversely though, I like the dry stream bed look with watery-type plants growing in it. So, how do I rationalize this dichotomy?

Someone more informed on the subject would probably say I was alienated from water in childhood – and when I remember being invited to 'come on in' to the North Sea in 'summer', I think that they would be right.

I have always enjoyed wider landscapes and the place of water within them – the glassy plane of a lake, or the chattering of a rushing mountain stream. Near my home now there are brimming clear chalk streams with strands of waterweed swaying in the current. Water on a large scale, therefore, I do enjoy – so proportion and scale help to determine my feelings.

I think that what I am saying is that I find the transposition of a 'natural' watery look – rushing or still – into a reduced garden setting difficult, and usually unconvincing, not only in its scale but also in its siting. Few ponds, obviously not positioned as nature would, seem correct, and as one of our basic elements water needs very careful handling in its surroundings.

Some years ago I wrote a book on Islamic gardens, spending time in southern Spain, northern India and Iran where I worked. In these hotter parts of the world and in the context of the Moorish and Mogul garden, I really saw how formalized water was used both functionally and symbolically on the palatial and domestic scale.

In my own designs, it is in the built environment where I am much happier with the use of water, no doubt because of this experience. However, the Moorish and Mogul water was always lit by the sun, and their fountain sprays sparkled and cooled the air. Of course, the same can happen here; but often does not because of our climate. Water used with the built environment is not, I believe, quite so dominant a feature, and I therefore find it more satisfactory to use it in this way.

At the end of the day, as a designer, one provides only what the client wants and what the site dictates. Personal preferences are not necessarily important.

People's attachment to the allure of water is often, I believe, almost mystical. For when it is tranquil, preferably with sunlight playing upon it, water has the power to calm; it is both restorative and contemplative. Again, I think that it is difficult to achieve on any small scale, although when trying to use it, in whatever its designed form, it is this criterion which I seek to achieve. The wrong fountain, the wrong rocks, the wrong planting may so easily destroy such a composition, which does not necessarily need decoration anyway.

Time and again I realize that while I struggle on with water detailing, nature gets it right every time in her simplicity. From her the designer and often the client, too, can learn a lot. It is worth a close study.

Isabelle Greene, Santa Barbara, California, USA

My practice originated in a dry part of the world where water is special, a precious jewel. In designing for this climate water is not to be lightly squandered but rather used in consideration of the whole environment. Thus I have evolved some unusual ways of including water in the garden.

One of these, oddly enough, might be termed dry water or the substitution of water-like elements. Often slate, pebbles or rock move in flowing patterns through my gardens, transforming themselves from pond edgings to dry creek beds, to stepping stones and trailing off into ribbons of strewn pebbles.

Sometimes slate paving reminds me of the desert floor, with sinuous patterns as if a flash flood has just evaporated, leaving its tracery behind. Concrete pathways with etched patterns suggest waves lapping or current flowing, leading the eye in a particular direction.

Of course, I often put 'real' water to use in gardens in a naturalistic manner. In these designs, the water and any associated materials form with,

The play of light with shadows and reflections activates this restricted space, designed by Isabelle Greene. The limited range of materials adds to the character of the garden.

and blend into, the existing geology, respecting the fact that real water always flows downhill, collecting at the lowest point. I take advantage of the large sandstone boulders that are indigenous to this area, to create naturalistic swimming pools, spas, pools, reflecting ponds, waterfalls and fountains. Swimming pools have become a popular luxury in southern California because of our rainless and pleasant, warm summers.

I also design intellectually with water as evident throughout history. That is, I use geometric or classic shapes and obvious man-made materials. Normally these designs would relate to a property laid out in a particular style. Wonderful old fountains or birdbaths from estates from bygone eras, as well as brand new elements of stark and clean design complementing contemporary homes, are often included as the garden design evolves.

Finally, I sometimes include water in a design as a clear, flat plane of relief where other elements have become too busy or distracting. There is simply nothing that is quite so still and serene as the beauty of a body of water.

21

Anthony Paul, Black and White Cottage, Surrey, UK

My love of water started when I was a boy in New Zealand. At the bottom of our garden we had a small stream, in and around which my brother and I spent hours playing. We made dams and bridges and all sorts of pools to make the stream more interesting and, of course, we fell in regularly.

As a garden designer, I became fascinated by the use of water in small spaces. Not that I ignore the large scale; in my own garden I have constructed three large lakes to surround the house with water. However, the skill in capturing the fun and excitement of water is something that takes time to master. In a small space water is essentially a magnetic attraction, taking centre stage and leaving most other garden features in the shade. Its tranquil sound and reflective qualities are its soothing properties that ensure that water is almost obligatory for the garden decorator.

In this garden designed by Anthony Paul, the links with the landscape beyond are clearly defined. The architectural qualities of the paving are softened by the textured, marginal planting.

Water in small spaces can be manipulated to suit the choice of garden style. I have used a ceramic artist to create a sea-horse fountain head decorated with large clam shells for a formal Italianate garden, or I have constructed a small wall fountain, covered in hand-made tiles and ceramic rocks to simulate cut stone.

In small gardens a water rill, although not a new idea, can run through the space and diffuse water throughout the garden or take advantage of level changes. Moisture-loving plant material, with strong foliage textures, can also be fed by the rill or grown in separate bog gardens to similar effect.

I have always been impressed by the way the Japanese designers have used water – normally just a hint of water in a bowl or trickling through a bamboo spout into a pond or container. I believe that there is great scope for invention in this area of design. Water pouring into a large glazed ceramic pot or over a simple flat stone and then into a reservoir below to be circulated are also ideas with potential.

The success of good water garden design relies on an observation of nature, other designers and earlier examples. Keep the design simple, use the best quality materials possible and make sure your technical knowledge is sound. If not, employ a specialist who can supply these skills. Water in the garden will provide hours of pleasure to repay good investment.

WATER IN THE FUTURE

Technology in the twentieth century has changed the construction of water features dramatically, with concrete, butyl, fibreglass and plastics now widely used. This, in turn, has revolutionized the way we design water into our gardens and landscapes. What is certain is that we should embrace these changes and see their true potential for bringing life, humour and spectacle into our lives.

The recycling and conservation of water are already important issues as we become all too aware of the fragile balance of nature. Reed beds for cleaning our waste water could, for example, soon become a regular feature of many gardens. Designing for wildlife is also a relevant trend, linked as it is to the preservation of endangered species. The suburban gardens of our towns and cities can easily be designed to attract and accommodate wildlife by the creation of habitats that mimic those of the countryside. Water plays an essential part in this approach, and the greater the variety of habitat that can be provided, the greater the variety of species.

The scope exists for a myriad of uses and applications of water within the garden, and it is the intention of this book to reveal at least some of them. What is more important, however, is that we should approach the subject with an open mind and aim to understand the design approach or the application to a given location.

chapter two

DESIGN CONSIDERATIONS

Once the decision has been taken to introduce water into the garden, it is essential to consider this element as part of the overall design of the garden. Without the development of an overall design concept, water will sit in splendid isolation as an uncomfortable extra forced onto the garden stage. This approach, which will work both for established and virgin gardens, should take account of a number of factors. Many of these influences will be picked up in an analysis of the site, while others are matters of taste and imaginative design.

SITE ANALYSIS

The site analysis takes account of all those existing factors that may influence the design and siting of any feature within the garden. Initially, these factors simply need to be recorded, and drawing a rough sketch plan may be useful here. The orientation of the garden must be noted because it determines which areas of the garden receive full sun, partial or full shade and at what time of day.

Sunlight and Shade
Identifying areas of light and shade is common for any type of garden design, but in deciding the design and position of a water feature it is essential. A pool in dense shade will be a dull affair and will not be conducive to healthy conditions for aquatic and plant life. Light energizes the system and also allows moving water to sparkle and attract attention. Partial or dappled shade provides the best of both worlds and lends character to water with the changing patterns of light and shade providing high contrast and a sense of movement.

This incidental pool is almost lost under the luxuriant foliage of hosta and iris. The informal treatment suits the shady location.

    Sunlight is an important element in the success of a water feature particularly for planting. Water lilies, for instance, enjoy warmth and in even partial shade will be much less likely to flower successfully. In those features that do not require planting the enlivening effect of sunlight in

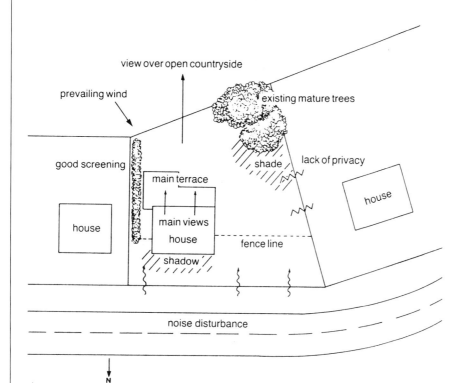

view over open countryside

prevailing wind

existing mature trees

good screening

shade

lack of privacy

main terrace

house

main views

house

fence line

house

shadow

noise disturbance

N

Drawing a sketch plan of the site will help in the assessment of the garden before the position of the water feature is chosen. In this example, locating the pool near to the house would seem to offer maximum enjoyment but might deter wildlife. A position close to the far boundary of the garden would be more likely to encourage wildlife but would affect the existing view. A decorative or ornamental feature near to the house or a soft, natural pool placed near the boundary so that its affect on the view is minimized are possible solutions.

catching water spray or moving jets is to be encouraged. However, there is the drawback, particularly in the design of pools, that too much sunlight will encourage algal growth, which will cloud the clarity of water, discolouring the features and reducing the chances that a balanced ecosystem will develop. Water lilies and other surface-leafing plants will shade the pool and thus reduce light penetration.

It is possible to combine some shade with water, and the effect of dappled light or the reflections of overhead tree canopies can be most appealing. However, the shade should not be dominant and the overhead tree canopy should not be too dense. The problem of leaf drop into the water in the autumn must be taken into account, for although floating leaves can be attractive, they build up as a deposit on the bed of the pool and can emit harmful gases, such as methane, as they decompose. This layer of humus will also, ultimately, promote vigorous plant growth and provide a medium for plant material to invade.

Soil Type

The lie of the land needs to be considered, especially if a close imitation of nature is intended. Water will naturally seek low ground or hollows, and to site a pool on top of a mound or rising ground may seem unnatural. The nature of the ground is also relevant because soils that are naturally permeable or that lie above permeable rocks, such as sandstone or limestone, are less able to hold standing water. Clay soils, however, will do this more easily. Close observation of the surrounding landscape will provide clues to help in the development of your design. This does not mean that a garden in a limestone area cannot include a water feature, just that the design of that feature needs to be carefully considered.

The Water Table

Linked to the type of soil is the level of the water table – that is, the naturally occurring level of water stored in the ground. The depth of this water level varies. In some areas it has dropped dramatically, either through climatic conditions such as drought or through the activities of man in exploiting water.

In other areas the water table may be high or even visible at the surface in the form of natural pools. There will also be seasonal fluctuations in the water table, which can sometimes be dramatic.

Ironically, a high water table can cause the most serious problems in pool construction. Because the level is not constant, the water-filled pool that is dug in autumn or winter may be a dry and cracked basin in the summer. Alternatively, an artificial method of construction, such as a butyl liner, laid in the drier spring or summer will bubble up or inflate as pressure from below builds up as the water level rises in autumn or winter.

This simple, reflective pool relies heavily on the play of sunlight on the Rudbeckia *planted alongside. This is a signature of the American designers Wilfred Oehme and James van Sweden.*

27

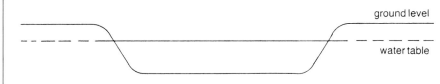

ground level

water table

The water table represents the natural level of water stored in the ground. This level, which can fluctuate considerably, sometimes dramatically affects artificial water features.

These points require a certain amount of local research, but they are essential facts that need to be considered in the early stages of planning. There are other environmental factors to take into account, such as prevailing winds, vegetation and local hard materials and their use, all of which will affect the development of a design in various ways.

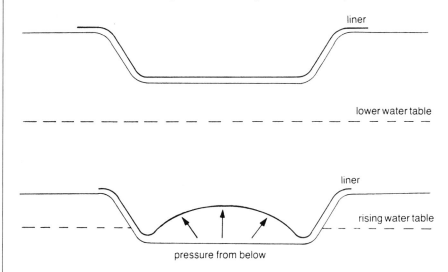

liner

lower water table

liner

rising water table

pressure from below

Pools built when the water table is low – during periods of drought, for example – can be seriously damaged when the water table begins to rise.

DESIGN ANALYSIS

The question that must be asked here is: 'Why is a water feature required?'

It may be that the sound of water is important or that the excitement of moving water is desirable. Both of these characteristics need to be enjoyed at close quarters, and siting water by the main seating area or terrace makes good sense therefore. Alternatively, the water may form a backdrop or an incidental feature to a quiet retreat somewhere deep in the garden. Such areas require a certain amount of privacy and shelter, which may already exist or may need to be created by screening with planting, trellis or structures of some kind.

Positioning your Water Feature

If the water is required to be a focal point in the garden its positioning needs to take account of the main views both from the house and within the garden itself. The final location may be some distance from the house, and the feature may become something to be visited or to be admired from a

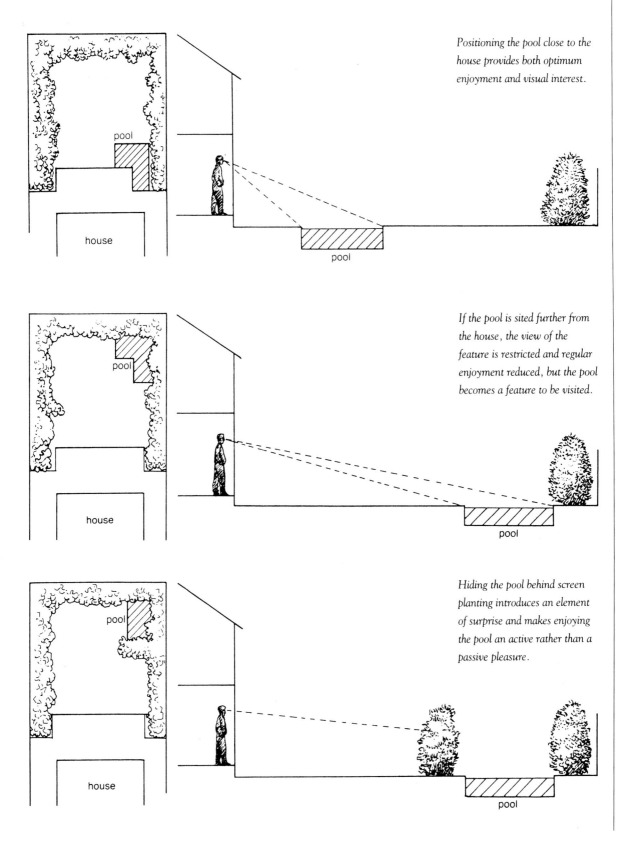

Positioning the pool close to the house provides both optimum enjoyment and visual interest.

If the pool is sited further from the house, the view of the feature is restricted and regular enjoyment reduced, but the pool becomes a feature to be visited.

Hiding the pool behind screen planting introduces an element of surprise and makes enjoying the pool an active rather than a passive pleasure.

pool

house

pool

pool

house

pool

pool

house

pool

distance. Using water to excite the senses or as a decorative focal point in a garden means that, in design terms at least, anything is possible. The feature may be outrageous or flamboyant, a source of fun or simply offering visual pleasure.

The attraction of wildlife may be of prime importance in including water in the garden. This presents something of a dilemma as a quiet, hidden pool will certainly attract most visitors but little will be seen. The closer the pool to the house, the fewer the species attracted to it. Using water to attract wildlife means that a re-creation or enhancement of nature is much more important to the success of the design and to the resulting habitat.

Water and Children

Children are automatically attracted to water, finding it exciting and distracting. All five senses may be stimulated by water in its many different moods, and generally water is great fun. However, if water is introduced into a garden with children specifically in mind, it is essential to consider their safety and it is best to locate such a feature close to the house so that any accidents can be dealt with immediately. Younger children, and toddlers in particular, fail to comprehend the dangers of water, and their eagerness to explore may lead to dire consequences. Large, deep expanses of water should be avoided, and the edge or bank treatments should be gently sloping, rather than stepped or steeply angled, to make escape much easier. Raised pools can prevent accidents as children have to climb into or up to the edge of the water. Planting around the pool might also help, but fencing, unless used as a temporary measure defeats the object of including water as a decorative feature.

Danger can be eliminated in other ways. Bubble fountains, which emanate from, and drain back into, an underground reservoir, provide sound and movement but the absence of standing water means that they are essentially safe. Other features designed along similar lines, such as taps draining into gullies, are equally effective.

Water for Leisure

Water for leisure and for fun introduces swimming pools, spas and jacuzzis into the garden. These are often included indoors, particularly in colder climates, but a hot tub close to the main terrace adds vitality and animation to the garden. Although these small spas can be covered when they are not in use, larger swimming pools can be difficult to disguise. There is a tradition of painting or tiling swimming pools in an unearthly turquoise, which strengthens their impact. Try alternative colours – dark green is much more appropriate, softening the impact and harmonizing with the general surroundings, and black, midnight or dark blue have good reflective qualities when the pool is not in use.

Water in the form of swimming pools, spas and jacuzzis, can be introduced into the garden for leisure purposes, but by painting this swimming pool black, David Hicks has created a reflecting feature which suits the recently planted avenue.

There may be any number of reasons for introducing water into your garden, but it is essential to identify them and put them in order of importance. A designer, for instance, works by establishing a brief that embodies the client's requirements, which are then listed in order of preference or importance to enable design decisions to be taken. If you are designing or creating a pool for yourself, the process should be the same.

STYLE

Having considered the historical context of water in garden design it is possible to see the range of design options available and to understand the potential of water within the garden.

Your choice of water feature should not simply be based on the fact that one style appeals more than any other but rather on the fact that the one you choose should be appropriate to your garden. However, the best rules are often laid down only to be successfully broken.

31

A Japanese water garden, for example, would suit more contemporary or modern architecture because the forms and lines or proportions are considered in a similar way. However, there was a great fashion for Japanese gardens in the Victorian era, and many of these, such as the one at Tatton Park in Cheshire, are now widely admired.

Alternatively, a formal style does not necessarily have to exist in a formal setting. Certainly, the general opinion would favour such a decision, because the resulting harmony would be less likely to surprise or shock the senses than a formal pool in an informal setting. Yet, many of the great British gardens owe their popularity to this particular combination of a formal, geometric layout and an informal overlay of planting.

There have been times in history when a specific style or system of design would be held up as a paradigm of virtue and perfection, a symbol of a way of life. In the late twentieth century, however, it is a case of 'anything goes',

The formality of this small pool suits this garden setting and creates a focus of attention. The corner blocks of yew frame the feature well.

for we are able to choose the style that best suits our way of life or, more often, our aspirations. While this allows a freedom of expression in design terms, the consequences can be confusing and disappointing. The discussion of style is important to the creation of water gardens, which should be considered as part of the entire design.

ARCHITECTURAL STYLE

In most cases it is the house or property that dictates the style of the garden. The sheer size of the building in relation to its surroundings is mainly responsible for this, but a secondary, and sometimes more important consideration, is the part played by the architectural style. However, styles do not need to be slavishly reproduced – indeed, from a creative design aspect this is not to be encouraged. William Robinson wrapped the informality of a wild garden around his Elizabethan mansion at Gravetye in Sussex, UK, without causing any serious concern about whether it was appropriate. Geoffrey Jellicoe sited a Surrealist garden in a Tudor setting at Sutton Place in Surrey to critical acclaim.

For a harmonious and satisfying blend of styles it is worth noting and following the nuances of architectural style. For contrast and excitement, however, it may be possible to break stylistic rules and to introduce alternative patterns and forms. In the Victorian era this style was termed eclecticism and, at its best, it produced inspiring combinations. At its worst, the results were confusing and preposterously over-decorated.

Whether or not rules are to be broken, a certain amount of unity in design is always welcome. The materials used should be limited to provide a link to the prevailing architecture. In areas where brick is common, it would make sense to use the same or a similar material in garden construction. In a central London garden a pool edged with London stock brick will look more harmonious than a pool in the same garden edged with Cotswold stone.

Other elements, such as the scale and proportion evident in the architecture of the site, should also be recorded and utilized. Patterns evident in architectural detail may suggest a concept or idea from which new shapes and forms may be developed to provide a unity of thought.

LANDSCAPE STYLE

In many cases the style or quality of the landscape has a bearing on design. The forms and patterns evident in the locality may influence and determine our preferences more than we might imagine.

This will be borne out in some areas more than in others. A town or city garden, for instance, allows more scope for experiment and theatricality in its design because the surroundings are man-made and artificial in a

recognizable way. The original landscape quality has been lost and provides no further influence on design style, save perhaps that of compatibility of materials.

Move further out of town and the sense of landscape style becomes more definite and a factor to contend with. The architecture and garden layouts produced by Sir Edwin Lutyens illustrate this point well. He preferred to use locally found materials that were in sympathy with the area in which he was working. His buildings and gardens are to be found in all corners of the world, and while the same hand can be seen to have been at work, the sense of place is undeniably unique to each example.

Thomas Church, the American landscape architect and garden designer, utilized the patterns of the nearby salt marshes in the evolution of his Sonoma garden and the pool, paving and lawns swirl and curve in unison.

Clear streams and waterfalls have their place in mountainous and hilly landscapes, but they are often introduced artificially into suburban gardens. The piles of imported rockery stone necessary to these features can frequently appear out of place, and these elements need careful consideration and deliberation.

Again, freedom of choice plays a part here but there are many alternative ways of introducing waterfalls and streams into a garden that can be equally rewarding and, perhaps, more imaginative.

GARDEN STYLE

At times the style of the garden itself may have a bearing on the design of the elements contained within it. The size of a garden is an important factor, for larger plots allow separate areas to be developed, each with an individual style or character. Those furthest away from the main house may take on a style of their own, completely independent of the rest of the garden or of the architecture.

This style typifies the early twentieth-century gardens of Vita Sackville-West at Sissinghurst Castle, Cranbrook, Kent, and Major Lawrence Johnston at Hidcote Manor, Gloucestershire. Both are organized as highly structured gardens, with hedges or walls used to enclose separate and autonomous gardens, each with a colour theme or particular function.

Obviously not every garden has this amount of space, but there is a general rule that gardens become less formal or structured the further they are from the main house. This approach would allow naturalistic pools in the peripheries of a garden that may be regular and formal elsewhere. Alternatively, a formal water feature may be adopted to emphasize the symmetrical nature of a garden layout when soft and luxuriant planting may partially obscure this quality.

Cottage gardens are typical examples of this approach. Although they often appear to be jumbled and relaxed in character, their basic plans are traditionally regular. The planting disguises this regularity to some extent, but a formal water feature will still feel appropriate, harmonizing with the organized layout and contrasting with the informal planting.

In general it is best not to think of the water feature you are planning as a new and separate addition to the garden but as an integral part of the overall design. If the entire garden is new, this concept is relatively straightforward. It is a much more difficult task when water is to be added to an existing design.

These various design influences should be used together in order to help in the development of the water garden. Once the general approach is developed and established, specific decisions may be taken in choosing the appropriate form of water for your garden. The following chapters investigate the various options in detail.

chapter three

POOLS

The pool, the simplest of water features, is created in a hollow or depression in the ground as a collection point for draining water. As is frequently the case, simplicity can be most appealing, and for still, reflective calm these features are difficult to beat.

Pools offer a haven to a variety of wildlife and are also functional. At one time, no farmyard was complete without its pool, travellers used village ponds to wash and refresh their horses, and dew ponds were once a regular feature of the countryside. In warmer climates water stands in pools less frequently, but flash floods or heavy rain produces a flurry of activity around a temporary pond.

Although many of these pools were naturally occurring features in the landscape, it became necessary to construct ponds to deal with increasing demands. In some areas, pools were created in holes or depressions carved out of non-porous rock. More generally, the depressions would need to be treated in some way to prepare the ground for holding the reservoir of water, and the most traditional material for pool construction was puddled clay. This material is still in use today, but it is becoming increasingly difficult to find and therefore more expensive.

In addition, using puddled clay is labour-intensive because the material needs to be introduced in thin layers. The introduction of new materials that serve the same purpose has made the world of the water garden accessible to many more people.

SHAPING A POOL

Even in small spaces, simple pools can introduce interest and vitality. This dark, reflective water surface contrasts well with the surrounding planting and paving.

In creating a pool it is important to bear in mind the simplicity of the original ponds. Water is unique as a material in the landscape and in garden design. The liquid will always find its own level and will echo the shape of the depression or hollow in which it sits. No other material directly responds to the contours or shapes of the landscape in this way. It is, therefore, essential that the shaping of a pool is carefully considered.

37

Informal Pools

The basic shapes are simple circles and ovals, although soft shapes formed from curved lines have a popular appeal and are frequently chosen for garden use. In addition the current trend for butyl liners as well as the puddled clay method of lining a pool suit this kind of shape.

The simplicity and definition of these curving shapes is particularly important to the success of the pool. If a pool shape is drawn out in the planning stage, use a compass to define the curves and measure the radii accurately. This will make its eventual building in the garden much more straightforward, and the arcs or curves will appear strong and elegant. These shapes suit wild or informal gardens, where the whole ambience is soft and relaxed. Planting along the margins of the pool will further subdue and disguise the overall shape.

Sir Edwin Lutyens utilized circles in his garden design to emphasize important features or pivotal points. Here, a simple lily pond is framed and accentuated by the paving pattern and the screen wall.

It is best to avoid narrow channels or pinch points in the layout of the pool. Such shaping will restrict water movement and could lead to stagnation, and because the depth of water will be reduced algal growth will be encouraged. This problem often develops when islands are introduced into pools. It is better to set the island well into the main body of the water so that the channel is sufficiently deep and wide to avoid these problems. The shape of the banks will also affect the depth and width of the pool in such instances.

Formal Pools

Obviously not all gardens fall into the informal or naturalistic category, and where formality is demanded clarity of shape is of prime importance. Squares, rectangles and circles or parts of circles are favoured as they are regular in nature and symmetrical.

The equilateral triangle, although a regular shape, is rarely seen, perhaps because of the difficulties in detailing. Generally these more formal shapes are defined by hard materials, either as an edge or rim or as a complete terrace of paving. Occasionally planting is included, but this is generally subservient to the strong geometry.

Dealing with Excavated Soil

There are numerous combinations of hard and soft materials and of shaping and styling in pool detailing that will produce the desired effect and the correct balance of formality or informality in your garden. In creating a pool, however, one major additional factor is frequently overlooked. Apart from raised features, which normally sit on or above existing ground level, all other pools involve excavation.

The quantity or volume of earth to be dug out of the ground may seem trivial, but even the smallest pool creates quite a mound of soil that needs to be considered as part of the whole design process. Added to this, excavated earth will increase in bulk by up to one-third, depending on the type of soil involved. This can have serious implications for the cost of the project, especially if the soil is transported away to be dumped. The overall budget is often eaten away by increased costs before any of the materials necessary can be purchased.

The usual response to this problem is to pile the earth into a heap alongside the pool to form a rockery or a waterfall complex, a solution that, if sensitively handled, can occasionally work but such a design frequently looks unnatural and out of scale with the rest of the garden. A more successful answer is to distribute the soil widely throughout the entire garden, but this serves to illustrate the need to see the development of a water feature as part of the overall plan of the garden rather than a simple addition or extra.

Size and Shape

Finally, the size of a pool and the position from which it is viewed directly influences the reflective quality. In general, garden pools tend to be small, and they are frequently tucked in at the end of the garden. There may be an element of surprise in such positioning, but the chances of enjoying any worthwhile reflections will be minimal. Perspective reduces the size of an object with distance and also flattens shapes, turning circles and curves into elliptical shapes and squares and rectangles into triangles or trapeziums, basically narrowing down the amount of water that can be seen. It is important, therefore, to consider the size and shape of the pool at the planning stage and to stake out the pool before finally deciding on the position, so that the shape can be considered from the main viewing points.

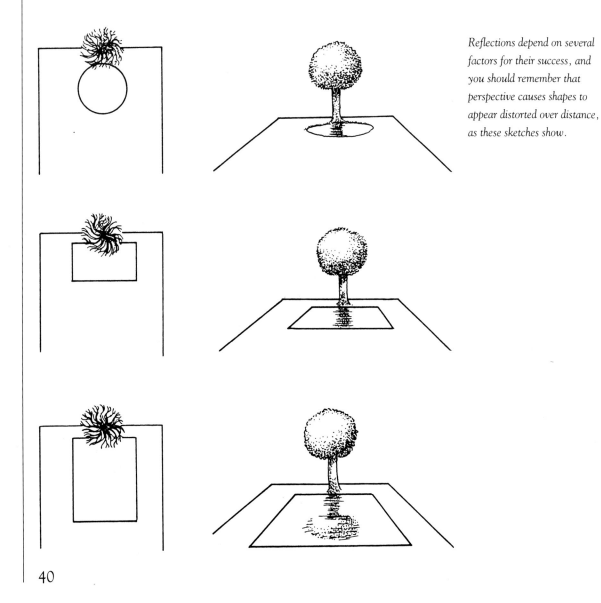

Reflections depend on several factors for their success, and you should remember that perspective causes shapes to appear distorted over distance, as these sketches show.

CONSTRUCTING A POOL

There are two methods used to build a pool: the rigid construction and the flexible construction. As a rule, the former is most appropriate to the hard, geometric pool, while the latter suits the soft, irregular pool. In fact, the flexible method of construction can be applied to almost any situation, and here cost or ease of construction may be deciding factors.

Rigid Pools

Rigid construction relies on the use of shuttered concrete, concrete blocks, brickwork or timber to create the basic shape or form of the pool. The structure, which may be either sunk into the ground or raised above ground level, would need to be waterproofed before water can be introduced and the finished detailing considered.

In general, rectangular or polygonal pools are made from these materials, largely because of the properties of the bricks and blocks or of the timber shuttering used for in-situ concrete (that is, concrete poured and cured on site as opposed to prefabricated concrete, which is formed elsewhere and delivered as a unit). This does not mean that curves and circles are not possible, merely that they are more difficult. If these shapes are preferred, the water feature as a whole needs to be a reasonable size and a simple shape. The tighter and more complex the shape, the more complicated and potentially expensive the construction.

Concrete This extremely versatile material is supplied in two forms. Most of us recognize the precast concrete that provides us with paving slabs and so forth. Its name refers to the fact that such material has been manufactured and formed to a standard dimension for use as a unit of construction. Apart from concrete block, it is not recommended for basic pool construction, although it is useful for the more decorative or ornamental effects for fountains, cascade details or spouts.

In-situ concrete is either delivered to site in a liquid, ready-mixed state or mixed on site. In order to obtain the necessary shape or form for

The rigid sunken pool is constructed of poured or in-situ concrete, which relies on a mould or formwork for its shaping. You should pour the sides as soon as possible after laying the base.

a paving to overhang and disguise the structure
b hardcore or paving base
c concrete structure to a minimum depth of 215–250mm (8½–9¾in)
d reinforcing bars or dowels

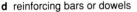

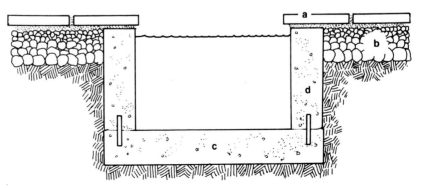

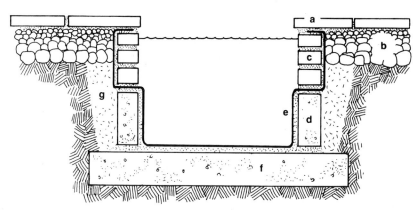

a paving
b hardcore
c brickwork
d concrete block
e flexible liner
f poured concrete base
g backfill

construction the concrete needs to be poured into a prepared mould, known as formwork or shuttering, which is normally constructed of timber. Much of the work involved with using this kind of concrete is concentrated on the design of the formwork. The concrete can be reinforced before the wet-pour stage, although regular garden features would not necessarily require this. Soil type and the final design of the water feature would influence your decision on whether to reinforce the concrete.

Precise construction with, or the correct laying of in-situ concrete requires craftsmanship and experience. This is particularly true of the formwork. Over large expanses or distances, expansion joints are necessary to enable the concrete to expand or contract with extremes of temperature without cracking. It is essential that specialist advice be sought.

Concrete block This is a form of precast concrete, and its use is becoming increasingly popular for the construction of rigid pools. The material is relatively cheap, and the large blocks are fairly easy to handle and quick to lay. Holes within the blocks also allow the material to be reinforced. Almost any shape is possible, although intricate patterns are difficult and often inappropriate. The material is not particularly pleasing to the eye, but the external face of raised pools may be finished with a more decorative material; the inner face must be waterproofed.

The side walls of this pool have been made from a combination of concrete blocks and bricks. The liner is taken behind the bricks for decorative effect, and this gives a much neater finish.

This pool has a poured concrete base, but the sides are built with concrete blocks. The flexible liner that has been used in conjunction with these has been tucked under the coping.

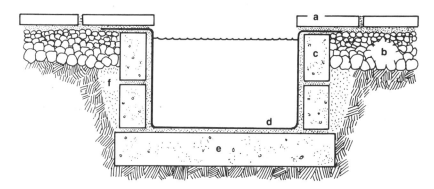

a paving
b hardcore
c concrete block walls
d flexible liner
e poured concrete base
f backfill/concrete

Waterproofing Waterproofing agents can be added to the concrete mix but visually the colour of the finished material needs to be considered. Both methods of construction outlined above benefit from the addition of a flexible liner.

Such liners can be made to measure, heat-sealed into box shapes and then dropped into place. This means that in-situ concrete in particular need not be perfectly finished because the surface will disappear behind the liner. Similarly, concrete block walls will be hidden by a black membrane, which removes the need to paint or waterproof further. Triangular timber fillets should be incorporated into the corners and angles of the pool base in order to make the final fitting of the liner neater and easier.

Raised Pools

Although containing water within a raised structure is obviously an artificial design solution, there are many advantages to be gained from this device. Disabled gardeners, for instance, benefit from the raised height, which brings water plants and the tactile qualities of water within reach. In addition, the level change allows water to cascade from high to low, creating waterfalls in a relatively restricted space. A height of approximately 450mm (18in) would allow the coping or the top of the retaining wall to be used for seating. This creates a talking point or a permanent seat in a terrace area,

These raised pools have been made of concrete blocks. The one on the left is faced with brick and the one on the right with stone. The liner in both is used in the same way as in the two previous examples. A height of about 450mm (18in) is appropriate for seating.

Poured concrete in formwork can be used for raised pools. The surface of such pools is often disguised with more decorative or sympathetic materials. Raised pools should always be reinforced for additional strength.

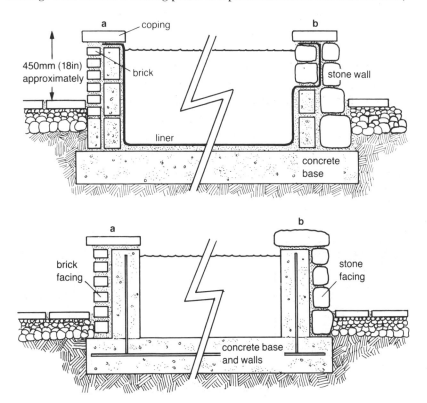

allowing people to come into direct contact with the water or with aquatic life as a source of interest and enjoyment. A workable width of coping would be approximately 300mm (12in); alternatively, the retaining structure could be designed to accommodate a seat or bench. Keep planting away from the immediate vicinity of the seat, as too much use may damage delicate foliage.

If the coping overhangs the wall on the pool side, it is worth filling the pool to bring the water up to a level just underneath. This keeps the waterproofing system out of sight and maintains the water as the centre of attention. A black liner or waterproofing treatment will make the pool seem bottomless and will allow cables or pipework to be disguised.

There is no specific restriction placed upon the height of a raised feature but once a container reaches 1.8m (6ft) in height the water will generally be above eye level and, therefore, out of sight. There may be a need for this kind of height for dramatic cascades or falls of water, but any other design quality is lost.

Almost any material may be introduced as a facing to the raised structure of the pool. Brick would be ideal but should be constructed as a double skin; stained timber would also prove suitable as a decorative treatment to a concrete or concrete block construction. Stone may also be used very successfully as a facing material over concrete block.

It may also be possible to build a completely separate structure around a prefabricated tank of glass reinforced plastic (grp) or unplasticized polyvinyl chloride (UPVC). The coping detail would need special attention, however, to ensure that unsightly gaps were hidden from view. Frost-proof tiles or mosaics can be introduced for vibrant colour effects, and glass building blocks would increase the reflective quality. Lighting can be used to great effect with glass building blocks.

Take care with railway sleepers, which will continue to weep creosote for an indefinite period of time and they should not be allowed to come into direct contact with the water. Some hardwoods, such as greenheart or ekki, will last well in water but make sure that no preservatives or harmful coatings have been added before use.

Sunken Pools

The rigid construction method can also apply to sunken pools, particularly in the vicinity of patios or terraces, where hard materials are dominant. Some of the most dramatic details of the water garden are possible in this situation. The architectural qualities of paving and walling can be contrasted with water and with the bold ornamental textures of aquatic planting. Simplicity of detailing is the key to success.

Paving should be allowed to meet the water directly, without any edge or coping detail. A cantilevered edge provides one solution, allowing the water

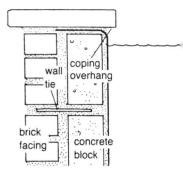

The coping material should, if possible, overhang the wall or pool side. The shadow produced helps to disguise the emerging liner and creates a neat finish. The water level within the pool should run just below the coping. Separate brick facings should be tied into the main structure of the pool.

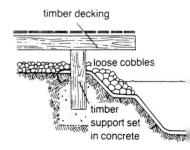

Timber decking next to the pool is particularly effective for disguising awkward details at the water's edge, and the decking can be easily cantilevered over the water.

apparently to disappear beneath the terrace. The last slab or brick is laid onto the containing structure of the pool but is allowed to overhang to create a shadow line, which hides this detail and the waterproofing system. The larger the paving unit, the larger the overhang within reason and balance. This works particularly well with timber decking, when the overhang can be exaggerated.

Stepping stones may be included, designed in a similar manner to create the illusion of floating slabs. By using the same material for both the terrace and the stepping stones, the terrace itself is extended across the water to provide a sense of continuity or at least a visual link into the main garden. Stepping stones or bridges are relatively easy to construct given the solid base of a rigid construction.

Because the pool is well below eye level, the treatment of the interior is vital. This may be darkened or painted if rigid construction methods are used or, as discussed above, a black butyl liner may be incorporated. The true depth of the pool may then become difficult to assess, and the reflective surface of the water may be used for decorative effect. Alternatively, the base or sides of the pool may be decorated with cobbles, for example, or for more colourful effect, with mosaic, but the reflective surface will then be of reduced importance. Lighting incorporated within the pool may bring these more decorative treatments to life and will provide a dramatic backdrop in the evenings.

FLEXIBLE POOL CONSTRUCTION

The traditional puddled clay liner is an example of flexible pool construction, where the waterproofing material follows the required shape or form of the water feature.

Lining Materials

More recently a wide range of flexible lining materials, geomembranes, has become available, and these are both cheaper to use and easier to install. The early examples, based on polythene, were relatively easy to puncture and often became brittle if they were in contact with sunlight. This meant that the edges of pools lined in this way became weak and leaks often occurred at these points. Technology has improved, however, and with the introduction of butyl these problems have virtually disappeared.

Butyl liners tend to suit softer, curvilinear forms or pool shapes. The banks of the pools need to slope for ease of construction, while the sides of rigid pools can be vertical. Acute or tight angular shapes are possible but difficult, and there is often a problem in bank detailing.

In order to contain the water, the liner must emerge above water level along the bank side. The quality of detailing here is very important, for an

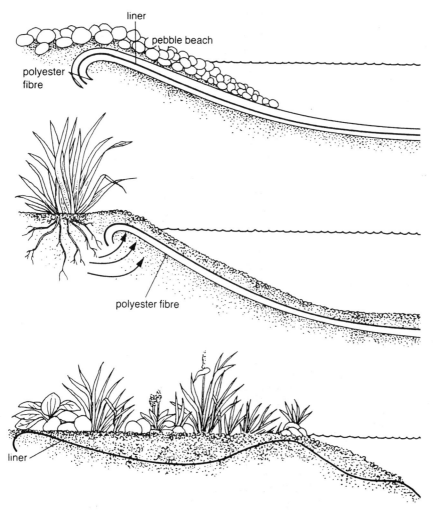

liner
pebble beach
polyester
fibre

polyester fibre

liner

Flexible liners can create difficulties when it comes to finishing off the bank because the weakest part in the construction is the point at which the waterproof layer emerges from the water to be secured on dry land. A pebble beach disguises the liner, but pressure on the surface can cause damage. A layer of polyester fibre both above and below the liner will reduce the likelihood of the liner being punctured, but this kind of material floats in water and must be held down.

Planting provides an alternative way of disguising the pool edge, but the roots of vigorous species can lift and puncture the underlay.

An excellent solution to the problem of finishing off the bank when you have used a flexible liner is to have a bog garden next to the pool, which secures the liner into dry land.

ill-considered design will leave the liner visible. This is also the most vulnerable area of pool detailing, not so much from the point of view of light degradation as from use. Pebble or gravel beaches can be easily disturbed, and planting can sometimes lift the liner with root movement or growth pressure. Polyester fibre underlays are now regularly used to prevent or to restrict this kind of damage. These woven membranes are manufactured in a variety of thicknesses or gauges to suit a range of applications.

Traditionally, sand has been used as a sandwich or buffer layer between the excavated ground forming the pool shape and the waterproof liner. However, sand disperses very easily, especially when the bank profile is steep, and, unless, it is held under pressure, it will slump or move with time. This can lead to an unnecessarily deep layer at the base of the liner, with virtually no protection in shallow areas. Ironically, this latter area needs the protection most, because access for maintenance, for example, puts downward pressure on the liner. It is relatively rare for the downward pressure of stones or pebbles used above the liner to puncture it, but stones or jagged material in the soil below can cause problems.

Laying the Liner

Once the pool shape has been excavated, a layer of underlay should be introduced to cover the extent of the pool, and it should be sufficient to extend over the margins to protect the bank. Almost any bank shape or gradient is possible with this method of construction. The gauge of underlay should be chosen with soil type and future use in mind. For example, stony soils or gardens in public use would require a greater thickness.

The waterproof liner is laid onto this base; again it must be large enough to cover the bank. The underlay, which is a protective layer, may be overlapped for larger pools, but the liner needs to be heat-bonded to produce waterproof joints.

Taking the adjacent soil and vegetation into the pool over the top of the liner gives a workable area that also helps to protect the liner. Building a planting shelf into the bank allows you to introduce marginal plants. The return mound or up-stand prevents soil from slumping into the pool.

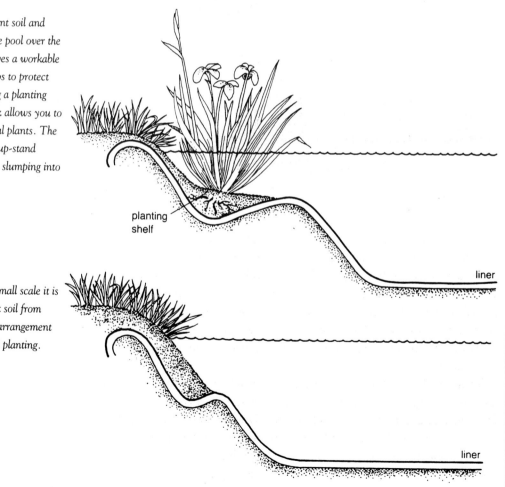

Even on a fairly small scale it is possible to prevent soil from slipping, and this arrangement needs no marginal planting.

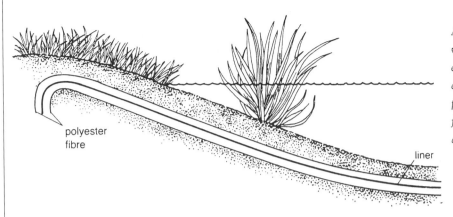

polyester
fibre

liner

A more gradual slope permits a variety of marginal and emergent plants to colonize the edge of the pool. An additional protective layer of polyester fibre is advisable, especially in areas that will be walked on.

The bank or pool sides may need further reinforcement. An additional layer of polyester fibre underlay to cover these areas can be useful because it will solve the problem of damage incurred during maintenance operations and will protect the liner from sharp and vigorous roots such as those of *Typha latifolia*. This top layer of polyester fibre could cover the whole feature but in most cases this is not necessary. In addition, the polyester floats in water and needs to be weighted down. It is possible to increase the gauge of the waterproof liner but this is a more expensive option, and it is best to allow the liner to hold water while the polyester fibre provides the strength.

Air pockets and creases need to be removed during laying, and partial filling with water as the work proceeds may help with this process. In the trade, these air pockets are referred to as 'hippos', because of their appearance if they break the surface. They can be the result of a fluctuating water table, as discussed in Chapter 2. Alternatively, air pockets trapped beneath the liner will have no means of escape or, more seriously, methane gas can be released from some types of clay soil to similar effect. Puddled clay linings will generally prevent this, although if the butyl is carefully laid it should solve the air problem without the extra expenditure on clay.

Gravel drainage under a liner can cause leaks. The leaking water needs to be redirected to a sump or soakaway. Sometimes a pump may be required to remove the excess water; alternatively, non-return valves may be fitted to the liner to release pressure. Clay, not necessarily high quality puddled clay, can be used on top of the liner. This technique weighs down the liner, provides a planting medium and improves the overall appearance. Where the water table is relatively constant, it may be possible to reduce the costs of constructing larger features by lining the sides but not the base. In effect, the pool stays full because of capillary action.

Shaping

The exact shaping of the pool should be dictated by its function. A simple reflecting pool will require the simplest detailing, and the bank profiles will be smooth and regular. A pool for planting, however, will need a number of different levels, shelves or planting pockets, which need to be prepared at the time of excavation. A beach of gravel will require a gradual gradient, allowing the water to lap and ripple along the shore.

A typical pool may include a variety of contours and ground formations to provide a varied picture or range of habitats once complete. A gradient of between 1:10 and 1:20 would provide a suitable shallow beach, while 1:3 or 1:2 would produce a steep-sided pool that would not be suitable for planting. Depending on the clarity of the water or planting density, it is possible to design a shelf with a shallow gradient that then drops more steeply further into the pool. This is particularly useful where space is restricted, and this sudden change of level will also serve to curtail plant growth and spread.

Planting can be included above the liner, although larger or more vigorous species may cause rooting disturbance. Soil pockets or mounds may be created specifically for planting purposes. However, once planting becomes established, there will be a production of litter and an accumulation of the growing medium on the floor of the pool into which planting may easily spread. Gradual bank gradients will promote the spread of marginals and emergent plants because these gentle slopes are easy to colonize and the litter layer builds up quickly.

The very edge of the liner is a difficult area as there is an immediate switch to dry conditions. A useful technique here is to extend the liner below ground level to create a bog area. The liner will create artificially poor drainage, and the moisture level can be topped up by a feed-in from the main pool. Effectively, this treatment creates a half-way house for planting between wet and dry conditions. Alternatively, the liner can be tucked down into the ground above the required water level, which means that a bank or mounded edge is needed. This kind of feature can look artificial and needs careful consideration in the early stages of planning.

Hard Materials

Hard materials may be introduced along at least some sections of the bank. There has been a great deal of poor advice given in respect of this kind of detail. It is bad practice to lay slabs or other paving elements directly onto the liner fixed with perhaps a thin bed of mortar. The support for such a detail will be extremely weak and may result in damage to the liner, cracking of paving or disintegration of the mortar bed. In addition, the liner is revealed above the water line to the detriment of the whole appearance of the pool.

This can be avoided by creating a low terrace around the edge of the pool, the base of which will be below the eventual water line. A concrete footing should be laid along the line of the shelf and the liner laid over the whole profile. Engineering bricks should be laid on the liner above the

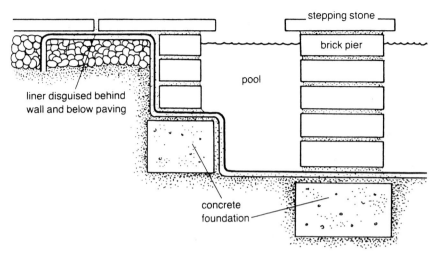

stepping stone

brick pier

pool

liner disguised behind
wall and below paving

concrete
foundation

*It is quite difficult to combine
hard banks and stepping stones
with a flexible liner. Concrete
foundations can be located
beneath the liner to support the
structures above, and the liner
can be taken behind the bank
wall and underneath the
adjacent paving. A column of
brickwork supports the stepping
stone; the overhang should not
be too great as this may
affect stability.*

footing to a finished height of a half brick above final water level. This
should be back-filled with concrete or hardcore and finished with the
required paving material. The slabs should overhang the brick wall to create
shadow and to allow the water to run underneath. Stepping stones should
be constructed using the same method, although the footing positions are
more difficult to establish and record exactly once the liner is laid. Crazy
paving is not recommended as a pool side paving material because an
overhang edge is difficult to achieve with smaller units.

An alternative method is to combine a pebble beach with a flat area of
paving. The pebble beach covers the liner edge and the paving is then
confined to dry land.

Pipes and Cables

Pipes and cables for fountains can cause problems both functionally and
aesthetically. In concrete constructions, these services are often hidden
within the fabric of the pool, and joints in liners can be waterproofed to
allow the pipe to run beneath the liner, emerging at the necessary point.
Otherwise, it is necessary to disguise these routes with pebbles, stones and
planting, while submersible pumps may be accommodated in recessed
cavities covered by a grill. Whatever the final outcome, it is important to
minimize this kind of disturbance and to keep all services in one duct or
route. This method also makes maintenance easier.

Rigid Liners

Rigid liners are widely used as alternatives to flexible liners, although their
preformed or manufactured shapes are not to everyone's taste and they can
be limiting in design terms. The cheaper versions are not strong and have a
short lifespan. Purchasing such liners to save money will probably prove to
be a false economy. It is also essential that both the overall depth and the

depth of the various planting shelves are checked before purchase.

The strongest liners are made of reinforced plastic or of resin bonded fibreglass. Choose the simplest shapes, as they will normally provide the surface area necessary for a healthy pond. The more complicated shapes are more difficult to gauge and to install.

DESIGN AND CONSTRUCTION

Size and Depth

There are two basic factors in pool design, size and depth, which must be considered in detail before the method of construction is finalized. In a pool with a surface area of less than 2.25 square metres (2.69 square yards), it will be difficult to achieve a balanced ecosystem. There will be more problems of algal bloom and of plant invasiveness or failure than in larger features, where the balance is easier to establish and to maintain. A minimum depth of 750–900mm (2ft 6in–3ft) of water is required for an optimum balance in the ecosystem. Planting will help to balance the system more successfully than any other element. It is often suggested that water snails will help to keep the water fresh, but they tend to eat the plant material.

Individual planting depths are given in Chapter 9. As a rule, however, submerged aquatics require a depth of 45–60cm (1ft 6in–2ft) and should be introduced at a shallower depth so that they can become established. Marginals need an average depth of approximately 20cm (8in), but any specific requirements may be accommodated either by mounding up soil or by basket planting, when the individual containers can be placed on blocks.

Plant Life

The plant life in pools takes out mineral salts suspended in the water. This is the basic food of algae and, once removed, the problems of bloom or cloudiness will recede. The various algicides now available act upon the mineral salts in the same way. Every pool will cloud up initially as the balancing process begins and the nutrient levels are adjusted. In addition, sunlight can activate the algae by warming the water. A sufficient depth will restrict this warming process, and water lilies or other floating plants will reduce the amount of sunlight entering the water. Submerged aquatics are probably the most effective oxygenators and help to keep the water clear, but they are also some of the most invasive plants as there are so few restrictions on their growth. The large-scale pruning of aquatics can lead to increased growth, just as hard pruning in the border will generally promote more vigorous activity.

In an effort to remove algal growth, the temptation is to drain the pool completely, in which case a return of the algal bloom is likely. In effect, draining the pool destroys the original ecosystem, and the new water needs

An unusual pool treatment at Preen Manor uses the decorative quality of cobbles, washed with water. Planting is restricted to formal positions around the feature and the overwhelming quality of the space is hard and architectural.

to be balanced again. A partial drainage is much more satisfactory, because the ecosystem will adjust more easily and more quickly. It is recommended that maintenance operations are carried out on a regular, annual basis. More frequent operations will disrupt the ecosystem too much, while anything less will lead to much more work and the possible destruction or stagnation of the pool.

In some pools an algal growth known as blanketweed may occur. In small amounts this weed will clean and clear the water body, and it is thus a valuable asset. However, it can grow out of hand and needs constant control. The best method is removal by hand, because although chemical control will certainly kill the plant, the resulting decaying matter may seriously reduce the oxygen content in the water.

Maintaining a Balanced System

Fish are not necessary for a balanced system, and many thriving natural water bodies succeed without them. In more sizeable lakes and ponds the larger fish such as carp will reduce vegetation growth either by feeding or by root disturbance. Fish themselves can greatly increase the need for maintenance as their waste can affect nutrient levels and chemical balance. In addition, most pools tend to be overstocked, which makes matters worse. The presence of fish may also affect the pH of the water because they produce carbon dioxide, which reduces the pH value. Too many fish will produce too much, and planting will be unable to cope with the excess. Unless fish are specifically required for ornamental or special interest, it may be wise to omit them from the pool altogether. Other factors such as rainfall, local water quality and the plant material within the water can affect pH. A value of 7–7.5 is the optimum.

Pools without vegetation are just as prone to algal growth. The depths given above should be maintained, although many designers are tempted to provide shallower features. Circulating water will restrict algal growth to some extent, although this only serves to mix the water together, preventing the top levels from overheating.

Filtration may also help to reduce algae in the system. The biological filters use bacteria that devour the algae, whereas pressurized sand filters simply act as a sieve and the algae are still present in the system. To achieve a 100 per cent clarity in pool water, a filtration unit one-third as large again as the pool surface area would be necessary and this would cause severe problems in any garden. Regular maintenance in the form of pool sweepers or skimmer boxes, which need to be cleaned out, are practical alternatives.

Overflows

Almost every pool will need an overflow to allow excess water to drain away. This volume can be quite considerable depending on the size of the feature, and ignorance of this simple requirement can cause serious problems. A bog section will act as a balancing area for excess water, but it is better to create a soakaway adjacent to the pond into which water can drain without causing flooding. Generally the overflow should be hidden from view, for most people would find this an intrusion and something which betrays the artificiality of the feature. In larger features the soakaway might lead directly into a watercourse or ditch, while in smaller pools it could be hidden beneath a pebble beach.

If you plan to build a pool overflow that leads directly into a watercourse or drain, you should check with the local water authority before installing such a system. Alternatively, the water can be neatly and effectively disposed of in a soakaway, provided the ground is not clayey. The soakaway should be at least 5m (16ft) from the edge of the pool.

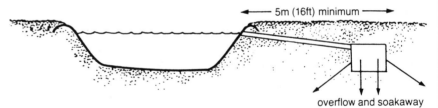

5m (16ft) minimum

overflow and soakaway

Bog Gardens

Bog gardens are easily constructed alongside the pool, but they should be considered at the planning stage rather than as an add-on feature. The flexible liner system of waterproofing is most appropriate to bog garden construction. The bog section needs an excavation of its own, with a mound of earth dividing the bog and the pool. The liner should be fitted over this mound, laid in the same way as the pool liner, with the top of the mound at or just above the water level.

The liner in the bog area should be punctured at the base to allow restricted drainage and the base should be covered with free-draining grit. The bog then needs to be back-filled before planting with a free-draining, but moisture-retentive, compost. It is important to remember that these artificial systems can dry out very easily in the summer, and extra watering may be necessary.

EXCAVATION

All but raised pools require excavation, and for those of any size this can be a major operation that needs careful prior planning. Initially, it is essential that the levels in the vicinity of the pool are ascertained. For larger features it is essential to carry out a full levels survey. Water will obviously find its own perfect level, and although the ground may appear flat, slight changes of level or gentle gradients may not be apparent. For smaller features, levelling can be easily rectified during construction, and the top of the bank can be checked once the main excavation is complete.

The outline shape of the pool is best decided on paper first and the basic outline can then be marked out in the garden. A system of stakes to mark the main points or outline can be used, supplemented by spray marker to provide an accurate digging line. It is often best to cut the turf along this line by hand first before any major excavation is undertaken. This ensures a clean edge to the pool once soil is removed.

In general, pools will have sloping banks, and the base of the bank, rather than the top of the bank, which forms the ultimate edge of the pool, should be identified with the spray marker. This will allow any errors in excavation to be contained within the final shape of the pool. Thus the feature should be excavated with vertical or near vertical sides, and the shaping of the banks should follow as a final detail.

For larger ponds, this method makes it possible to use machinery or plant on site to carry out the bulk digging without the possibility of causing any serious damage to the final shaping. Use tracked vehicles at all times to minimize compaction and soil damage. The banks may be formed by dragging the soil down into the excavation, which is easier than pulling the soil up on to the bank side. The latter technique can also damage the surrounding garden. For all excavation work, safety must be taken into account. This is particularly important for depths exceeding 1m (3ft 3in), for in such cases there is an increased chance of soil collapse.

Sizing the Liner

When you order the liner, you should measure the length and breadth of a feature in its entirety – that is, the base of the feature plus the bank depth on either side should be allowed for. In addition, allow an extra 500mm (20in) minimum on these measurements or 1m (3ft 3in) maximum. This will provide enough liner to overlap the banks and to be anchored in trenches around the perimeter of the pool. It is essential also to leave sufficient liner at the edges to allow for the downward drag that occurs as the pool is filled with water. On wet soils this can also lead to compaction of the ground as filling commences, which results in reduced bank heights and problems with water retention.

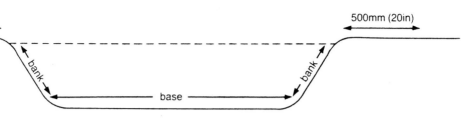

500mm (20 in)   500mm (20in)

bank   bank

base

When you are ordering or measuring the liner, add together the base and both bank dimensions and allow an extra 500mm (20in) all round the pool to accommodate fixing details, stretch and movement.

Disguising the liner as it emerges from the water to dry land is the most difficult area of detailing, particularly in naturalistic settings or alongside grassed areas. The gradient of the bank can be manipulated to some extent by creating a 1:2 gradient for lining purposes. This may then be overlaid by clay or excavated material (depending upon the quality) at a shallower gradient, say 1:3, which then appears to be a continuation of the bank into the water body. Problems may arise with this technique because the soil tends to slump into the water at the base of the slope. Including a lip approximately half-way up the bank covered with the liner, holds the soil or clay more permanently. These methods of overlaying are particularly useful when a high water level is desired.

Islands

If islands are required it is best to consider their positions before excavation begins. These features should be lined and detailed as for any section of the main bank. If islands are created during excavation, they must be built up in layers of 150–200mm (6–8in), and each layer must be compacted as construction proceeds. Islands laid on the liner will exert undue and damaging pressure, which can lead to serious ruptures of the liner.

For larger pools it will be necessary to join separate sections of liner together. Adhesive can be used, usually a contact type, but a cold-weld tape will do the job just as easily. It is important that the liner is cleaned beforehand in order to obtain the most successful and long-lasting joint. White spirit is a useful cleaning agent, drying quickly before the tape is attached. If it is applied in colder weather, applied heat will promote a successful bond. (A hair-drier will suffice.) Specialists use a hot-weld system, which relies on plates at a high temperature to seal joints.

Cheaper liners are more difficult to join or to patch because the materials do not respond in the same way as butyl. These lower cost materials should not, in any case, be used for larger features because they will not withstand the pressures and weight of water. The weight of any liner, particularly those required for larger pools, should not be underestimated. It may take one person to excavate and to remove spoil in loads from the pool, but the liner will need to be manhandled into position and transported to the site, and you should make sure you have help at this time.

chapter four

STREAMS

I n the natural landscape still, reflective water is represented by the pool or pond and, although these features can exist independently, they are frequently linked by moving water in the form of streams or rills. The addition of sound and movement in the flow of water is always attractive and appealing. Rivers and streams draw our attention, they fascinate and mesmerize us with their liveliness, and we romanticize about their journey through the landscape. We go in search of a source, tracing narrow channels back to springs and lakes. We are attracted to busy ports and estuaries where the rivers meet the sea, and we imagine far off exotic places.

It is no surprise, therefore, to find streams in our gardens. They can be used effectively to link different parts of the garden, providing a sense of continuity or movement between different areas. A backdrop of sound or moving, flickering water will provide a constant element or feature against or around which a wide variety of plants or hard materials may be arranged.

Conversely, streams may be used to separate different areas within the garden. Such a decorative form of definition is both welcome and suitable, obviating the need for walls or hedges, which may prove too oppressive or solid. In a similar way, streams can be used for increased security, as a 'safe' barrier, rather like a moat, to dissuade unwelcome visitors.

Streams vary in character from slow-moving, almost stagnant channels covered by bankside vegetation to lively, shallow mountain courses where the water is clear enough to see every stone on the bed. It is possible to recreate these characteristics in the garden, but the resulting features should either match or boldly contrast with the required mood of the garden.

The depth of a stream is variable and will depend upon the overall

A simple oak bridge crosses the water in Anthony Paul's garden in Surrey. The planks sits just above water level, providing an exciting route between the luxuriantly planted banks.

appearance and on the speed of flow. A shallow, fast-flowing stream on a smooth bed will provide a strong sense of movement and will sparkle with light in the right conditions, but there will be little evidence of sound. The rill at Rousham House, Oxfordshire, a garden by William Kent (c. 1685–1748), uses this technique to good effect, contrasting smooth curves of fast-flowing water with the planting through which it runs.

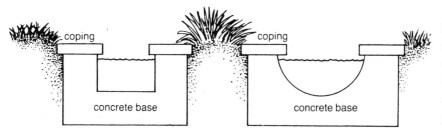

coping   coping

concrete base   concrete base

Rills can be simply built in in-situ concrete or by using the techniques illustrated on pages 41–3. Use paving to form a coping or edge detail or to provide a mowing edge.

By introducing obstacles and textures into the stream bed the water will dance and leap to produce sound. Regular placement of the obstacles will create uniform rhythms of movement and sound, while irregular arrangements will create rapids and eddies in the water, a variety of flow that is fascinating to observe.

Shallow streams will permit decorative treatments of the bed to be considered and enjoyed. Colourful pebbles, cobbles and rocks may be introduced, the colours of which will be intensified by the water and the quality of light.

The stream at Shute House, designed by Sir Geoffrey Jellicoe, changes in character as it flows through the garden. Here, the water runs in a shallow bed, revealing the cobbled base of the channel.

Deeper streams tend to be associated with slow-moving water, and they lend themselves to wild or woodland gardens where they benefit from additional planting. Slow-moving streams may be included in a garden as a secondary feature that is discovered by surprise or simply as a means to introducing wetland or moisture-loving plants into the borders. Fast-moving water should not be planted, because the growing medium will be swiftly eroded and, in any case, most water plants prefer still or slow-moving conditions.

Gertrude Jekyll and Edwin Lutyens made good use of these features in some of their gardens. At Hestercombe, Somerset, there is a narrow channel or rill with tiny circular pools created alongside to accommodate water planting. At the Deanery, Berkshire, the planting is contained within the channel itself, allowing the spiky leaves of iris to punctuate the manicured lawns alongside. Although these gardens are large in scale, the ideas can be translated and adopted for much smaller spaces.

It is a useful exercise to commit your ideas to paper before constructing a stream. No matter how rough your drawings, the opportunity to realize potential difficulties or to avoid mistakes is invaluable. A plan will be useful for plotting the course of the stream bed and for showing which areas of the garden are to be linked. A simple cross-section through the middle of the stream will also prove useful in allowing you to understand the gradient or shaping of the stream bed.

In general, a slope of 1:30 should be seen as a maximum gradient. Anything steeper will cause the water to move too rapidly, producing potential pump problems which will be discussed later in the chapter. For any reasonably ambitious schemes it is best to consult a specialist designer or constructor.

The essential attribute of water in stream flow is that it moves. In nature this characteristic is part of the overall circulation of water around the planet. Helped by gravity and gradient, the water finds its way from the highlands to sea level and, as long as there is rainfall and evaporation, this cycle continues.

In the garden, unless the site is blessed with a natural stream, there is a need to re-create this movement. Otherwise, although there may be a natural gradient within the site, it will be necessary to pump the water from the lowest to the highest point by artificial means. This involves a system which relies on an external source of energy, usually electricity, which needs as much consideration as the stream itself and will be dealt with later in this chapter (see pages 64–5).

As with pools, streams as water features fall into two distinct categories. Those that are designed to look 'natural' or to imitate nature and those that are obviously artificial, decorative architectural features such as the rills of Jekyll and Lutyens.

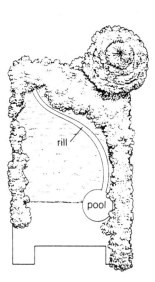

Losing the source of the rill in dense planting allows the sinuous line to emerge and edge a main border. The rill should drop into a simple pool, from which the water can be pumped back to the source.

59

CONSTRUCTING STREAM BEDS

The same basic methods of waterproofing pools outlined in Chapter 3 should be used in the construction of stream beds. For those schemes that aim to imitate nature, the rigid construction of concrete or concrete block is inappropriate because the shapes or forms required would be too complex. A series of cascades may be possible, and this will be dealt with in Chapter 5.

Rills

Concrete is much more suitable for the creation or construction of rills. These features tend to be more regular in design than the 'natural' streams and also tend to have a continuous uninterrupted gradient. They may be straight, like those on the terraces of Bodnant Gwynedd, North Wales, or they may have a serpentine form like that which runs through the planting at Rousham House, Oxfordshire. They are simple and straightforward to construct, and their obvious artificial nature makes them appropriate to the modern garden. Because they tend to be shallow, the water appears to move swiftly, but they can take the form of sluggish channels that may also take water planting. In the past they have often been used to link separate water features or to create long, narrow water gardens, such as those at Hestercombe, Somerset.

The rill at Hestercombe is one of the garden's most stunning features. The stone edged circular pools feed off the central channel, providing niches for water plants.

The rill may be constructed and finished in concrete, or brick or stone may be used for decorative effect, perhaps to match materials already in use elsewhere in the garden. In such cases, the decorative materials would be used as a facing or surface dressing on a concrete foundation. Their use may be purely decorative, perhaps to run alongside a terrace or pathway or even to run across paving, almost like a river needing a ford or stepping stones to facilitate crossing.

The main drawback in the design of the rill is the difficulty in retaining water should the feature be turned off for any reason. The fast-flowing,

A series of weirs along the length of a stream bed keeps water within the system even when the pumps are switched off. When it is circulating again, the water flows over the obstacles, creating sound and interest.

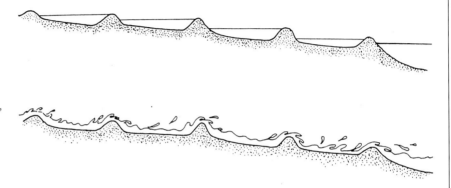

continuous gradient features require a holding pond at one or both ends of the system in order to store water when pumping is suspended. One solution is to build an underground storage tank, but the expense can be prohibitive and the water is out of site when the system is not in use.

In other systems, a series of weirs or dams needs to be designed into the system to hold the water within the stream when the pump is turned off. This means that the holding pools at each end of the system are not necessary because they are built into the stream bed, and the feature becomes a series of moving pools with rapids or cascades to accommodate the changes of level. These regulatory design considerations are essential to prevent flooding or the loss of water that might occur when the system is not in use.

Brooks

For a more natural effect, the liners discussed in Chapter 3 are most suitable for waterproofing the stream bed. Butyl, used in combination with a protective underlay, is easy to cut or shape into almost any arrangement. Achieving the effect of a meandering, babbling brook is a straightforward exercise as long as the sheets are completely covered. The stream will be much shallower than a pool or pond, and the bed will be visible. Pebbles or larger gauge gravel is best for this purpose, but fine materials should not be used as they will be eroded or washed out of the stream and into the pumping system. The judicious placing of larger boulders and stones over the changes of level and along the banks will disguise the sloping, liner-covered profiles. Plants may also be introduced into the pools, where they will become established providing the current is not too disturbing. Marginal and bankside species will soften the hard materials and help to camouflage the liner edge.

Detailed profiles or forms are similar to those of pools. A shallow dish or bowl shape will lend itself to softer planted edges, and a design with a deeper, flat bottom would enable rocks or boulders to be included to disguise or decorate the banks. The gradient is not too important, because the waterfalls linking the pools will accommodate the changes in level. It is possible to build a series of almost flat beds that will still function as a stream once the water is pumped around the system.

The use of rocks and boulders in stream design needs careful consideration. It is not simply a case of ordering rockery stone from the nearest supplier. Investigate local rock types and, if possible, visit the supplier. Large rocks have individual characteristics, and particular shapes or forms might lend themselves to either bank use or bed use. More rounded shapes are suggestive of water-worn forms and are often appropriate for placing on the bed of a stream to disturb the water or to narrow its passage. More angular boulders will be suitable for banks and shore lines.

Either rock type can be used for waterfalls, but they will produce quite different effects. Slate and granite boulders tend to produce sharp, distinct edges, which provide dramatic falls of water. Limestone provides softer forms for subtle effect and bubbling or tumbling water. The rocks can be used to create weirs and waterfalls or to decorate and sometimes form the path or route of the stream itself.

OPPOSITE Streams introduce moving water into the garden, with endless possibilities for stimulating the senses. Simple changes of level break the flow of water, instantly creating incident and attracting attention.

These cross-sections through stream beds show how rocks can be distributed across the water course. Generally, rounded pebbles or cobbles should be used under water, while rugged boulders can emerge from the shallows. Randomly placed boulders, on the other hand, will disrupt the flow of water and create drama and movement.

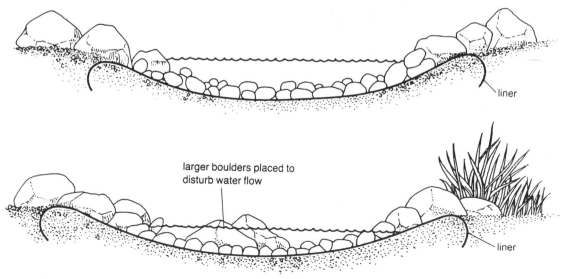

liner

larger boulders placed to disturb water flow

liner

The waterproof layer might extend to a width of 2m (6ft 6in), for example, while the water body may only be 30cm (12in) wide. The stream may appear to meander and play in a random pattern, dictated by the placing of rocks as obstacles. The remainder of the waterproofing should be disguised or shaped, but the placing of rocks or boulders should not be limited to the extent of the liner. A stream will seem to belong to the landscape if the materials are allowed to combine and coalesce. Thus planting may be introduced in and around the stream, and rocks or gravel can be drawn out into planting beds.

The liner itself does not need to be manufactured as one long piece, although this is possible. Each pool along the stream can be treated as a self-contained unit, and the liner should be long enough to overlap into the next pool. Laying should proceed from the lowest to the highest level to produce a watertight joint and overlap with the next pool up. The base of each pool should slope back from the weir in order to hold water.

Problems can occur if the liner is simply overlapped between lower and higher levels in the stream bed. This is particularly so when the stream design allows for pools of standing water. When the stream is at rest and the water level in each pool is at its highest, water may seep between the liner overlap. It is best to seal the joints with contact adhesive or cold-weld tape as discussed on page 55. The joint should be a simple overlap, which causes less tension within the liner itself and there is a reduced likelihood of splitting along the joint.

This method of construction allows each section of the stream to be unique, whereas the use of prefabricated units restricts and regularizes dimensions. The base profile of such units is also often unsatisfactory because they provide insufficient depth to accommodate the pebbles and stones needed for disguise.

Gunite is another material that lends itself to use on free-form shapes. This is a sprayed concrete in which the water is added to the other elements of concrete at the nozzle through which the material is forced. This is a highly specialized method of construction and requires specific skills.

PUMPS

There are no definite guidelines in stream design, but there are a number of considerations to bear in mind. Water has to be pumped around the stream system and a source of energy is required to serve this purpose. Electricity will provide this source and will be taken from the supply to the house. Siting a stream system close to the house would, therefore, make sense because the voltage reduction over great distances can be a problem. In smaller gardens this represents no great difficulty, but in a larger plot, positioning a stream at the end of the garden may need to be reconsidered.

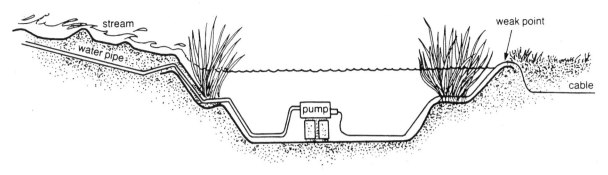

A submersible water pump, which can be placed directly into the water, is the simplest kind to use. Make sure that the pump is kept well away from any aquatic vegetation, and raise it from the floor of the pool on concrete blocks or bricks.

Ambitious systems will need large pumps to cope with the increased capacity and switching on a large system can be a sudden drain on the household electricity supply, leading to potential loss. It is worthwhile considering the alternative of a number of smaller pumps working together on the same system.

In the event of a system failure, it is likely to be the servicing that needs attention. Apart from the aesthetics of the stream design, it is important to consider the ease of access to pumps, cables and pipe runs in order to solve problems with the minimum of disruption. A separate access chamber alongside the water course is recommended, which should additionally serve for regular maintenance. In sizing the pipe work for the supply and return of water, it is best to choose the largest pipe affordable.

Submersible Pumps

There are two basic pump types, submersible and surface or external. The submersible pump sits within the water body and in terms of plumbing is self-sufficient for a water supply. The water is simply sucked in through a basic filter and expelled in the desired form, either as a stream or a fountain. It is important to keep aquatic plant material away from the intake, however. They emit very little noise, and the main difficulty is to disguise them when they are placed in the water.

A submersible pump placed in a separate access chamber is easy to maintain. The chamber should be fed directly from the pool so that the pump is always submerged. The top of the access chamber can be disguised with planting, or, if is sited on the main terrace, a recessed cover will take the necessary depth of paving.

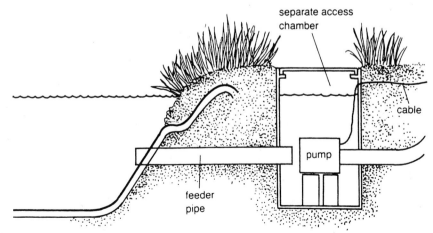

Capacity can vary enormously, and it is essential to choose carefully when specifying. A waterfall with a regular flow over a 15cm (6in) width would need approximately 3,000 litres (660 gallons) of water pumped through per hour; a 30cm (1ft) width needs approximately 6,000 litres (1,320 gallons) per hour; a 60cm (2ft) width approximately 12,000 litres (2,460 gallons) per hour. This would give a continuous sheet of water and a worthwhile fall over the weirs. If the stream feeds from a pool, the flow rate should be 100–150 per cent of the volume of the pool. Detailed flow information for a uniform depth of water over a 15cm (6in) wide weir is provided in the table below:

Depth of water in mm/in	Water in litres/gallons per hour
6mm /¼ in	545/120
12mm /½in	1,535/338
25mm /1in	4,363/960
50mm /2in	12,344/2,716
100mm /4in	34,913/7,681

The pump should be set above the base or bed of any pool, perhaps on blockwork. This prevents silt and sediment being drawn into the system. Pipes and cables may be taken over the waterproof liner to prevent rupturing the material, but all cables should be buried in a protective conduit at least 450–600mm (1ft 6in–2ft) below ground. It is this necessity which creates a weak point in the system. An alternative is to flange a hole pierced in the liner to take the cable out to the required depth, but leakage can occur using this method.

It is important to record the routes of cables and to mark the trench where possible. In addition, for safety reasons, it is essential to protect the system with a circuit breaker (residual current device or RCD).

Surface Pumps

The surface or external pump allows for longer runs or greater height differences and access for maintenance is direct, without the need to drain the system. These pumps have to be housed in a separate chamber to protect them from rain and freezing temperatures, and these housings need some design consideration or camouflage.

The pump should be sited as close as possible to the pool or reservoir, first, to keep pipe runs as short as possible and second, to enable the suction hose and strainer, which draw water from the pool, to work effectively. Some models of surface pump are self-priming and these may sit alongside the water feature.

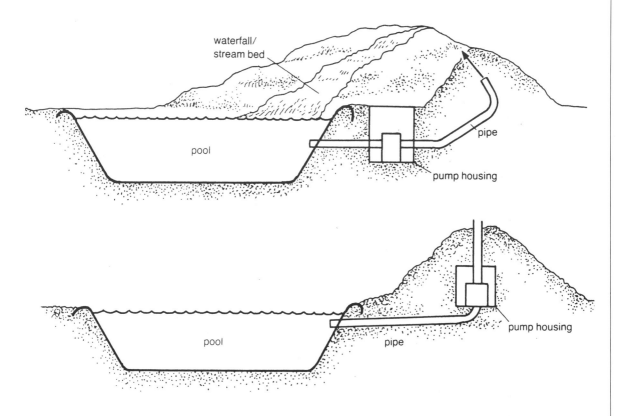

waterfall/
stream bed

pipe

pool

pump housing

pool

pipe

pump housing

A surface pump must be sited in a separate chamber, which may be located below ground level to permit a gravity-fed water supply. This kind of pump tends to push the head of water more successfully than it sucks from the pool. If the surface pump is located alongside the pool it can be disguised by planting or mounds of earth. Surface pumps are relatively noisy.

Placing the pump lower than the main reservoir level creates a flow of water under the force of gravity, and this provides a constant stream to ensure that the pump never runs dry. This is known as flooded suction. Valves can be fitted to cause the water to flood through the pump in this way, but the gravity system is much more reliable. The intake pipe should be one size larger than the delivery pipe because water is pumped out of the system more efficiently than it is drawn in.

Pumps are rated according to their capacity, and their output is determined by the head – that is, the distance from the outlet or stream source to the surface of the main pool or base of the system. Basically, the higher the head the lower the output. Long pipe runs will also affect this performance. There are many factors that can affect these figures, such as pipe diameter, length of run or width of stream. Before purchasing the necessary hardware it is worth seeking specialist advice.

All pumps should be fitted with a T-piece, which allows water to be diverted from the main flow. This is particularly useful for pond maintenance when the pump can be used to drain water from the feature. Filtration of the water within the system is also important, because organic matter or silt can cause serious problems. This may be a simple mesh grille designed to take out the major blockages, but it needs to be cleaned at regular intervals.

CROSSING WATER

The need to cross a river or stream in order to reach the other side is a basic instinct, indicative of our innate curiosity. In a design sense it also allows us to introduce and manipulate structures or facilities to make the crossing of water possible. This can be a most exciting and interesting development from introducing water into the garden.

Stepping Stones

At the simplest level, stepping stones provide such a facility. Their precarious nature makes them attractive to us, as we have to concentrate on the experience of crossing water. Obviously, this can backfire and the stones could easily become too dangerous to use. The surfaces should be non-slip or textured if possible, and the more regular the stones or slabs, the safer the crossing will be. The distance between the slabs is also a factor in safe use.

Rocks and boulders may be used, but their shape and form must be carefully considered. Large slabs can be embedded directly on the stream bed, where their weight should provide stability, although it may be necessary to use concrete haunching to provide a firm base and long life.

More sophisticated examples may be constructed using a brick pier topped with a variety of copings to form the stepping surface. The result of this method of construction means that the stones may appear to float just above the surface of the water especially if an overhang is allowed.

The sizes of the stones and the gaps between may vary to some extent. A good minimum size for individual stones is 450mm (1ft 6in) square; anything smaller than this may cause difficulties with balance. Gaps of 150–200mm (6–8in) between slabs would be workable, although this dimension is more variable. The average stride is approximately 600mm (2ft), and this should dictate the centre of each stepping stone or slab. The space between the slabs will vary with the type of material chosen.

You can either unify the materials using regular slabs with regular paving or achieve more dramatic effects by using regular slabs with irregular paving or setts and vice versa. The key to success with these more difficult combinations is to be bold and definite so that the contrast of shapes and materials is a central point of the design – there is no room here for half-hearted measures.

Stepping stones can be used dramatically along or above changes of level in the stream, allowing us to see rushing water at close quarters. The base of cascades is also an exciting location, where there is just a chance of getting wet. If possible, allow the stones to appear to be the only obvious means of crossing, perhaps by disguising any other route. In addition, the same slabs or materials can be used to create stepping stone pathways on either side of the crossing itself. This provides continuity in the use of materials.

Bridges

Bridges, the most common means of crossing water, vary from the simplest examples using timber lengths or stone slabs to the most elaborate edifices with arching spans and decorative railings or balustrades. Again, the surroundings or setting should influence your decision. Timber planks will suit a woodland garden and a stone slab a simple suburban garden. Save the chinoiserie for public parks and gardens unless the style suits and is appropriate to your chosen themes.

It is not always necessary to construct a full bridge as decks or jetties can provide access to the centre of a water feature without stretching to the opposite bank. For smaller pools and streams, the bridge footings can be based on the banks, with a single span bridging the gap. Longer structures for larger water features need more careful consideration because the main supports need to stand on the waterproof lining. Lighter structures can be set into concrete, which rests on the liner itself, but an alternative and stronger solution is to set down pads of concrete before laying the liner, and these can then be used as firm bases for construction without destroying the waterproof seal.

Larger structures should be discussed with specialists as they can produce heavy loadings and are relatively complex to design and construct.

chapter five

JETS, SPOUTS, FOUNTAINS *and* CASCADES

The sense of movement and excitement evident in a tumbling stream or a gurgling brook is infectious and attractive. However, for an inspiring and sensational approach to creative design with water look no further than the jets and spouts that have been used to decorate our gardens for centuries.

The Romans first manipulated gravity when they created water jets, and since then the sky has, almost, been the limit. Manpower, horsepower, steampower and electricity have all been used or abused at various times in the generation or creation of water spectaculars. In 1681 Sir Samuel Morland experimented with water jets at Windsor Castle, Berkshire, and successfully forced water to a height of 24m (78ft). He failed to convince Louis XIV of the efficacy of this system, and the Machine de Marly, which included 14 water wheels and 253 separate pumps was installed at Versailles.

Few of us have the space to enjoy such extravagant displays, but the drama of forced water is indisputable. The visual senses are entertained by the constant movement and the ever-changing patterns of sparkling and shimmering light. The sound created by this movement is no less stimulating and offers a complete distraction for our minds. The design opportunities available through the use of these features are myriad, and, unlike those installed at Versailles or Windsor, may provide a source of pleasure in even the smallest of gardens.

JETS

Ferns, ivy and iris surround this mysterious and atmospheric cascade. The hint of fossilized remains sinking into the dark water is both appealing and thought provoking.

Jets or similar features may be completely independent of any accepted water feature such as a pool or channel. In fact, in smaller or restricted gardens, this may be a positive advantage. The source of water to feed the jet may be located in a reservoir hidden below ground, normally beneath paving or a mesh, which might support gravel or pebbles. Water emerges under pumped force to rise to a predetermined height, which may be adjusted for greater or lesser dramatic effect.

71

With such a feature there is no evidence of standing water, which makes it ideal for children. They can enjoy the thrill of playing with the jets and fountains without coming to harm. Systems can be designed to allow close inspection of the water enabling us to walk through a light sprinkler shower or to dodge between individual jets of bubbling water.

Including timing devices in the pumping system makes it possible for individual jets or spouts to jump into the air or to cross from one container to another. This has been used to entertaining effect in various theme-parks, where small jets of water are ejected at carefully controlled intervals to seem to leap around from one pool to another like homeless caterpillars.

The jets can be reduced in pressure to provide bubble fountains, which disturb the water's surface so that it resembles boiling or simmering liquid. By placing the outlet of the bubble fountain just below the surface of a pool or container the whole surface may be activated and enlivened. Alternatively, the same system could bubble up through cobbles or pebbles, as if the water were erupting from the earth like a latent geyser or spout.

Jets are normally seen providing vertical displays of water, but there is no reason why the same fittings cannot be directed horizontally to emanate from a wall or similar solid structure and to land in a catching pool some way off. The cannon-like fountains at the head of the Trocadero water feature in Paris work on this principle, sending powerful arcs of foaming water into the pools below. These wall-mounted features are developed from the basic garden tap, and this device may be manipulated to provide larger-than-life torrents of water suitable for children's play or delicate streams to dribble into a sink or trough.

LEFT Sound and movement can be incorporated into restricted spaces, often disguising background noise. This drilled stone is washed with a small jet of water which then drains through the cobbles to be recirculated.

RIGHT The traditional water spout is given an amusing treatment in this incidental water feature. Textured planting helps to disguise the background and frames the feature itself.

These features work well in small gardens where space is restricted. It is common to see a variety of animal faces or masks designed specifically for the purpose of spouting water into a suitable container. The spouts do not need to be purely figurative, however, and good effects can be obtained with more abstract designs or shapes. The possibilities for using wall-mounted sculpture in a wide range of hard materials are almost endless.

Water can be forced through a wide variety of nozzles, allowing the jets to change in character, rather like adjusting the sprinkler device on the end of a garden hose. By flattening the jet a calyx of water is created, forming a clear dome of shining liquid. Forcing water at high speed through a fine nozzle or rose head produces a fine mist, which drops gently to earth, catching rainbow colours in the sunlight. Nozzles can be grouped together to produce flower heads of water rather like an umbel.

FOUNTAINS

Fountains may be introduced purely for fun, and they can be swivelled and directed if desirable. The fountain pool in front of the Pompidou Centre in Paris contains weird and wonderful creatures and forms, each ejecting water, turning with the wind and spraying unwary passers-by. In some of the water theme-parks in the United States children can play with jets of water around a shallow collecting pool. Obviously a warm climate helps, but the idea illustrates the point that water can be a source of pleasure in many different ways.

CASCADES

Cascades can be used in a similar way so the water drops vertically from one level to another, perhaps disguising an unsightly surface or counteracting unwelcome noise from an external source. By creating an entirely new cavity within or in front of a wall, water may be pumped up to spill over and back into a plunge pool below. Any number of containers can be used in a similar way. Huge pipes, pots or barrels will hold the pump mechanism or spout while water appears to bubble effortlessly from below, spilling over the top and down to a hidden reservoir or collecting pool below.

In contrast, a thin film of water may be spread over a surface or artefact to enhance the qualities of the material. The colour or grain of stone is often intensified or clarified by this technique, and metal surfaces shimmer with light and movement. Surface textures will direct or deflect the route of water, and although staining or surface deposits may occur, they may be used to decorative effect. Bronze works particularly well in this respect, and a surface patina is developed over time so that many different surface qualities may be evident in the same cascade.

A more dramatic idea is to direct jets of water to a higher level. If the jets are placed close together at regular intervals, the effect is similar to a cascade, but the water appears to defy gravity in moving from a lower level to a higher level. The water is simply collected at the higher level and allowed to drain back to the lower level. This may be designed to be invisible or the water may drain back as a curtain of falling water behind the jets of rising water.

Containers of differing heights could be arranged to allow water to drop from one to the other and may be used to form wall-mounted or free-standing features.

Richard Huws played with water as a mobile medium in his kinetic sculpture, the Tilting Fountain, sited in Liverpool. The fountain is made up of a group of different sized buckets, which are fed with water. As the smaller buckets fill, they tilt, spilling the contents into larger buckets, which, when full, empty in turn to create turmoil in the pool below.

Another possibility is to use chains to guide smaller cascades back down to ground level. This idea has been used effectively in housing design, where the chains guide water from the roof gutters down to drainage points, a more elegant solution than drainpipes. Stainless steel proves particularly effective for this purpose, as the shine of the metal adds to the sparkling effect. The chains must be held taut and vertical, or the water will find the shortest way down.

In streams and rivers cascades are evident as waterfalls or rapids as a water course changes level. The natural lines of these features are difficult to interpret, but the irregularity and random quality that attracts us is possible to approximate. The main difficulty in introducing such features into the garden is that they seldom look appropriate to the overall character of the setting. Frank Lloyd Wright created Falling Waters, Pennsylvania, a stunning residence cantilevered over a waterfall, where cascades and still pools form part of the overall structure and fabric of the building. Relatively few of us live in mountainous or hilly districts where such features may be possible and plausible. Straight copying in a suburban garden requires a tremendous suspension of belief. If this character of falling water is required, it is possible to use brick, appropriate stone or even timber to disturb the water flow sufficiently without having to import rockery stone that is not indigenous to the area.

By utilizing these various elements within an expanse of water, the resulting disturbance of the surface may be manipulated to enhance the design. The effects may vary from complete distortion and violent activity to serene ripples, rolling intermittently across a quiet pool. The play of light assumes a great significance in such a design, and in shallow water the pattern of ripple shadows or any form of surface disturbance can have a spectacular and mesmerizing impact.

Water playing in a series of jets and spouts introduces a sense of vitality into Anthony Noel's London garden. The careful positioning of decorative pots and watering cans adds to the amusing effect.

INSTALLING FOUNTAINS AND JETS

Installing a fountain involves relatively technical construction but the impact on the garden is dramatic. For many, the sight and sound of a simple fountain is enough, but there are many other exciting possibilities in this area of water garden design. Almost anything is possible but it is essential to work within the dictates of the site. It is dramatic but impractical to install a 10m (33ft) high jet in a small urban garden for example and, similarly, a simple bubble fountain would be lost in a large lake.

The pumps that make the water movement possible are similar in detail to those used for streams discussed in Chapter 4. They may be submersible or surface mechanisms, but the exact capability and choice of pump relies on the type of feature you wish to create. Fountains do not need to rely on an obvious or visible source of water to be effective. It is common to associate these features with pools or ponds, but water can associate well with hard materials, either flowing over the surface or erupting through paving from below.

Fountains or jets are best suited to formal pools as there is a direct contrast between the artificial forms and the random patterns of moving water. In more natural pools, this effect is lost, and the presence of a decorative jet or spray can seem alien and awkward. In addition, many designers find the combination of the downward movement of water in a stream or waterfall is at odds with the upward movement of water in a fountain. This is a common combination in many gardens where the problem is compounded by a reduced scale. Water can be controlled and directed in a variety of ways, but the overall style or sense of the design must be considered. For a quiet, restive effect a waterfall or a fountain may be enough, but the two together may be too much unless space is unlimited. For a lively and dynamic effect, jets may collide, dance or shoot off in numerous directions, but this would not be suitable in a natural or contemplative setting.

Fountains no longer have to describe a single jet of water soaring up into the air. A wide range of forms or patterns is now available, dictated either by the pattern or form of individual nozzles or by the arrangement of a group of nozzles in a particular pattern. Nozzle systems that spin are also possible to make the water jets dance or gyrate.

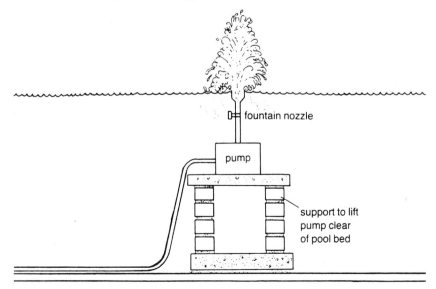

fountain nozzle

pump

support to lift
pump clear
of pool bed

A fountain and its associated pump can be placed together. The pump must be raised so that it stands clear of the pool floor and does not become blocked with silt. If this makes the pump visible, it can be sited within or below a feature that disguises it.

A separate access chamber next to the pool makes maintenance much easier, but the installation is much more complicated and extra sealed joints in the liner will be needed.

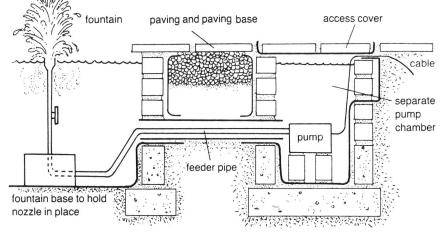

fountain · paving and paving base · access cover · cable · separate pump chamber · pump · feeder pipe · fountain base to hold nozzle in place

Submersible pumps will now fit neatly into the pool alongside the fountain nozzle so that they are almost unnoticeable once the system is activated. This will keep unnecessary and expensive piping to a minimum. The use of underground water reservoirs makes this kind of system even more attractive because the functional elements are kept well out of sight while the decorative elements catch the eye. There are a number of complete systems now available, and these are ideal for use in smaller gardens or alongside the terrace. The water and pump unit are held in a waterproof container below ground level while the fountain nozzle emerges through a protective grille. The grille may be covered in cobbles or small boulders, over which the water runs on its way back down to the reservoir ready for recirculation. It is possible to construct these features using butyl or even concrete. Millstones are often used to decorate these systems, with the water emerging through the central hole. Bubble fountains are perfect in scale and impact for this kind of treatment. Some of these features are available as fountains within free-standing containers. Although this idea may be appropriate for a balcony or roof garden, it is inappropriate for a standard application where the buried features are much less obtrusive, especially when out of action.

For a more dramatic effect, the water may be aerated filling the jet with foaming bubbles and white water. Placing a number of these nozzles close together in a simple pool provides an exciting centrepiece or focal point and may be used to contrast with dark reflective pools. By placing a simple barrage device around the fountain at surface level, the rippled or agitated water can be retained while the rest of the pool remains reflective.

It is important not to overdo fountain design. A single jet or bubble will provide sufficient interest and activity for the majority of settings. A complex of jets or a complex jet needs space and careful placing for best effect. Larger scale features work best when seen from a distance or in a large expanse of water.

In a more restricted space, powerful jets and violently moving water may introduce drama but the surrounding garden may be rendered useless once the fountain is active. This may be especially so if the prevailing wind and exposure within the garden space is not considered. In windy conditions it is possible for the jet to blow horizontally to at least its own height. This could mean a serious loss of water which could easily damage the system, particularly the pump.

When you are installing the fountain, the jet or nozzle should be positioned so that it protrudes just above the level of the water. The pump and fountain unit can be placed on supporting blocks or brickwork to achieve the desired height. In smaller pools this construction may be visible and it may be necessary to disguise the pier with stones or boulders.

Alternatively, the pump and nozzle or jet could be separated to reduce the bulk immediately below the fountain. The pump can be tucked into the bank or beneath overhanging decking. In all cases, the pump should be positioned well away from plant growth and lifted above the base of the pond or water feature. The removal of the pump to the pool side or even to a sunken access chamber makes maintenance and checking much simpler.

It is important to include separate control valves for any fountains so that the final height of the water spouts may be adjusted individually. The control valve must be related to the pump specification, otherwise the pump may easily be damaged. Ball valves are cheaper, but gate valves, which provide better control of water flow, are probably more effective.

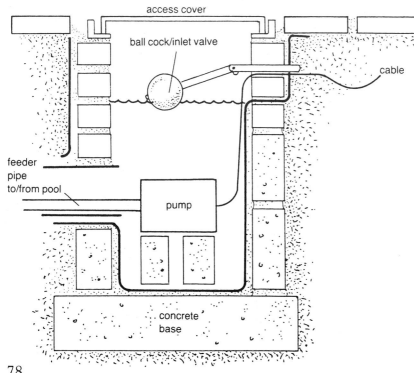

If you have a separate access chamber you will need an automatic top-up sytem to make sure that the submersible pump never runs dry. A simple ball valve will allow water to feed in as necessary.

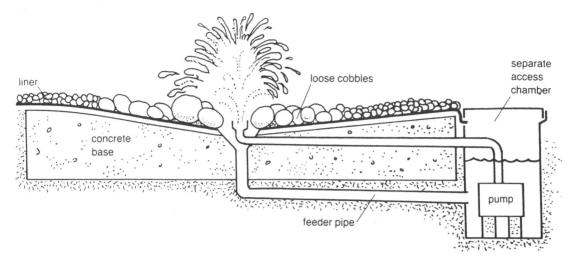

Fountains can emerge through paving, and such features are easy to maintain and can be swept or hosed clean without the need to maintain or support a large body of water. This detail shows a concrete base with a recessed route for pipe work. The whole surface is covered with decorative cobbles, and the liner can be folded back to give access to the feed and drainage pipes when required.

For fountains that are independent of a pool or stream bed it is necessary to construct a separate container or waterproof liner. Such features tend to operate from a reservoir below ground level into which the fountain water drains. In this respect, the sunken bubble features, mentioned earlier, work on the same principle. However, the force and quantity of water used in these features can be considerably increased.

Adequate drainage, underground storage, jet and pipe size and pump specification should all be referred to water or fountain specialists. The resulting construction, particularly of rigid features made, for example, of concrete, should also be handled by a designer or engineer. Flexible liners can be used, but a reinforced or solid foundation beneath the lining may be necessary because weight loadings can be significant. This technique of combining materials can have benefits, however. The concrete base can be constructed to contain pipework housed in conduits within an open trench, which is then covered and disguised by the liner. The liner can be easily folded back as necessary for any maintenance or servicing without having to break out solid concrete, a disadvantage with the rigid systems.

A more complex construction requires a subterranean tank to store the water needed to feed the system, while a pump supplies the force required to project water through holes in the lid of the tank. Surface water drains back through these holes and recirculates. A concrete surround provides a base for paving material such as granite setts.

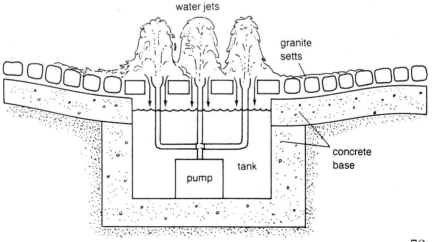

79

The same technology and construction advice relates to cascades and waterfalls. Although these features may relate to streams and water courses, cascades can be used as free-standing features in the same way as fountains. Unlike fountains, however, some kind of structure is necessary to create the cascade drop. The pumping mechanism is required to lift water to a higher level against the force of gravity to create the necessary effect. This may be a naturalistic feature that relies on a disguise of the necessary plumbing with ground contouring and planting. This is a similar design result to the stream beds discussed earlier.

For a more dynamic result, the water can be lifted vertically within a structure, such as a wall. This involves constructing a vertical pool, with the water retained within a constructed box. Rather than a typical, free-standing wall with a minimal gap betwen the two skins of brickwork, therefore, the gap between would be opened up and lined to contain the water. By forming a lip at the top or by slightly reducing the height of one side of the wall, the water will flow out and down the face of the wall. Alternatively, the water may be piped back up through the wall into a trough running along the wall's length. The trough would then act as a holding reservoir from which the water cascades. The waterproofing of this system is much less than is needed for the double-wall arrangement.

Engineering bricks, slate or lead flashing can be used to form the lip, which would help to throw the cascading water clear of the face of the wall. Protruding stone or brickwork on the face of the wall could be used to break up the smooth flow of water, creating disturbance and splashing.

OPPOSITE This lively cascade is created with a series of clay ridge files, placed to catch water on the change of level in a stream bed.

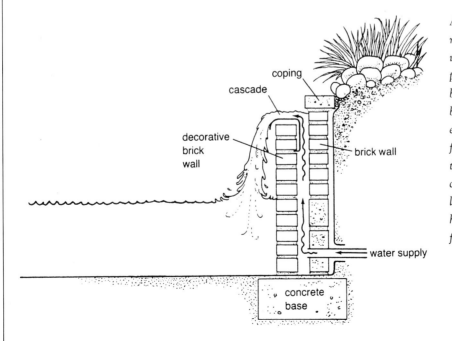

decorative brick wall

cascade

coping

brick wall

water supply

concrete base

A water wall is an effective but relatively complex feature for use next to a pool. Water is pumped into a vertical space between two separate skins of brick- or blockwork and emerges at the top of the wall, from where it gushes down over the shorter of the walls. A coping of stone, slate, tile or lead flashing on this wall will help to guide and control the flow of the water.

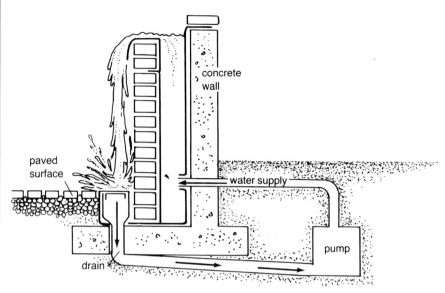

labels: concrete wall, paved surface, water supply, pump, drain

A free-standing wall of concrete with a separate facing wall of brick gives the same effect but can be used as a stand-alone feature. The water falls into the gully or drain and recirculates via the pump.

In any cascade, the edge or lip over which the water must flow is an important element of design success. A smooth, flat surface or edge will produce a steady flow of pure, clear liquid. A contoured or shaped lip will force the water into a jet or spout, and a rugged or rough surface will disrupt water flow to produce drips and eddies. Japanese designers greatly prize the stones and rocks that create these varied effects, even to the extent of seeking out stones that appear to carry a cascade when no water is present.

An alternative to the vertical cascade is a sloping or stepped feature, in which the water is either contained on a series of regular levels or is forced down a gradient at speed. The effect of the water can vary from a mere drip to a torrent to produce a transparent glaze over the hard materials or to create a white waterfall of froth and excitement. It is important that the edge of the cascade is absolutely flat to ensure that water spills evenly over the edge.

In colder climates the effects of frost and freezing temperatures can ruin or at least damage water features, particularly those such as fountains, streams and cascades, which rely on pipes and pumps for effect. In many countries it may be necessary to drain the pipe network in winter to prevent damage from the expansion of water. This is probably the easiest of the options available, although the feature can then be enjoyed only in the summer months. Alternatively, the fountains or cascades can be left running permanently, although for private use this may be considered a waste of energy. An alternative option is to use heavier gauge piping. Thick-walled medium density polyethylene (MDPE) pipe is capable of taking high pressures, and acrylonitrile butadiene styrene (ABS) piping will also take greater pressure than the more generally used UPVC pipes. The thinner the pipe wall, the greater the chance of split or rupture with freezing and thawing. Valves are often the weakest part of the system and a great deal of freezing damage occurs here rather than within the pipe itself, with additional problems being caused by the fact that many of the materials used in manufacture will corrode. Stainless steel fittings are available, and they have a long life expectancy, although they are more expensive initially.

In general, do not use simple hose fittings. Their capacity to carry water is restricted and their life expectancy is short, although their flexibility is an advantage sadly lacking in the variety of rigid pipes available. Ninety-degree turns, for example, should be avoided and are, in any case, virtually impossible with these rigid materials. When you are excavating trenches, therefore, this should be an important consideration. Keep changes of direction to gentle curves and try not to use junction units for sharp turns, because they will dramatically reduce flow.

In the UK at least, there is a general confusion between pipe and fitting dimensions. A 63mm (2¼in) outer diameter pipe will provide a 50mm (2in) core diameter (internal dimension), and a 90mm (3½in) outer diameter pipe will provide a 75mm (3in) core diameter. The fittings in general are still manufactured in imperial sizes, which creates problems at the junction points. These pipe sizes are expensive, and although smaller diameters may be possible, those mentioned will provide a strong and free flow of water. Generally, costs increase as pipes increase in diameter.

Flexible pipes can sometimes move or flex as the water flows through them, and this is a particularly important consideration if pipework is unsupported. For example, millstone features or bubble fountains cannot be constructed with surrounding pipe support. It is often advisable to use rigid piping for these features. Heavy elements, such as millstones or boulders, can also crush a flexible or narrow gauge pipe and so restrict the water flow. Whatever the pipe and fitting specification used in the construction, it is important to make sufficient allowance in the costing and planning stage.

In addition, pools as well as pipes may need some kind of buffer to prevent damage to the structure of the liners or walls. A hollow rubber tube around the edge of a retained pool is a useful addition in the winter months, particularly for those features with an overhanging coping where the expanding water or ice can become trapped.

Free-form pools where there is no such bank restriction do not suffer in the same way because the water is less confined.

chapter six

POTS,
SINKS *and* CONTAINERS

Pots or other containers that can hold water are often sold as the ideal solution to the small garden or terrace. In fact, there is no reason why large water features cannot grace a small garden. In reality, this is just the manipulation of stark design contrasts that, if handled well, can be successful. Although scale and proportion are often cited as defence against such extremes, a bold approach to design can pay off, and the greatest errors of judgement are usually made in choosing features that are too small for a large space rather than vice versa.

Decorative water containers such as pots, sinks or barrels should be chosen on their own merits. They should be seen as decorative items for the garden or as focal points, adding a small glint of light or colourful reflections. The water within may be used for extra effect, as an additional surprise element. The technology is available today to line and waterproof almost any type of container.

The idea of contained water is as old as gardening itself, but the first examples would have been functional. The conservation of rainwater in some kind of reservoir is still with us today, showing the value of this basic concept. The Romans used stone cisterns or tanks to store rainwater, but later these were made of lead or cast iron. The tanks were usually rectangular, but many different alternatives were developed to suit the fashion of the day. Ornamentation in the form of scrolls, swags, faces and arabesque scrollwork abounded, and these garden antiques are now prized collector's items.

The Japanese used a variety of containers to collect water for their garden ceremonies. The *tsukubai*, or water basin, was normally a low circular stone with a central carved dish designed to hold water. Visitors had to crouch or bend to wash in the water, thus humbling themselves in readiness for the tea ceremony. At the same time, a scene would be revealed to reward or surprise the visitor. The water would be allowed to overflow into a gravelled or pebbled surround, and larger but subservient stones would complete the arrangement of objects to provide balance and harmony. Often, odd

This simple, stone sink filled with cobbles provides an unusual, incidental feature for a town garden. The clipped box spheres add texture and visual interest.

85

OPPOSITE *The Japanese water basin, or 'tsukubai', can form a perfect focal point in even the smallest garden. To create the right effect, the materials and planting used with such features must be sympathetic to Japanese design philosophy.*

numbers would be used in such arrangements; threes, fives or sevens were most common as they made it possible to achieve a balanced design without the need to resort to symmetry, and this same preference may now be found in contemporary western design when informality is required.

In Europe, old barrels or stone troughs were often used to collect rainwater or to water the traveller's horse on the village green. Often pumps would be installed, with some kind of catching container for overspills. It was not long before these features became adopted for a decorative rather than functional role in the garden.

They are still popular now as relics from the past and put to many different uses. Lovers of alpine gardens follow a trend begun in the 1920s for using old stone sinks, and these features are now highly prized. On this small scale, the soil conditions can be easily altered to suit the selection of plants to be grown within the trough. The same principles may also be applied to their use as water features.

If there is insufficient room or if it is too difficult to construct a pond, a low trough or sink is an ideal alternative. In a relatively small space, such a container, once filled with water, will introduce reflections, water planting

Even the smallest water containers can provide interest. This bird trough introduces a splash of reflected light to catch the eye in passing.

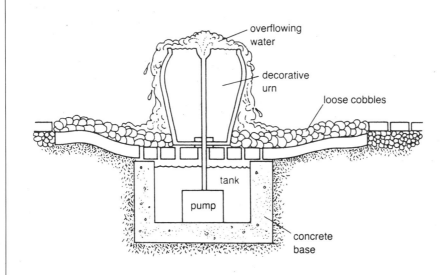

overflowing water

decorative urn

loose cobbles

tank

pump

concrete base

Decorative pots or containers can be used to hold bubble fountains, spilling water over the sides and onto the ground below. A hole is drilled in the base of the container and then sealed so that water can be pumped from the storage tank below, which can be disguised with pebbles or gravel.

or, possibly, a small bubble fountain. Water circulation or the inclusion of oxygenating plants will keep the water clear and fresh. The feature can be raised above ground level for decorative effect or buried into the soil, in which case the container itself is less important in decorative terms and may therefore be much cheaper. Barrels and half-barrels are also very effective containers as well as being extremely resilient.

Pots or containers can be used effectively as incidental features within the garden, where they may be stumbled across as if by accident. If the container is carefully selected, the contrast between foliage and artificial form may be emphasized. Choose large, obvious containers for this purpose because once the pot is in place, the disguise offered by the foliage will reduce its impact and effect. A simple, shallow dish will prove ideal for this purpose, perhaps set into low groundcover. This will also attract the birds, thus introducing extra life and movement into a corner of the garden. Alternatively, a large urn or tank will provide an architectural mass to balance individual specimens or groups of plants. Make sure, however, that the container is not so high that the water contained within it is hidden from view.

As focal points in their own right, containers should be special or significant in some way. This does not necessarily mean that the feature should be particularly decorative, but it should be capable of attracting attention and should look appropriate in the chosen location in terms of proportion and style.

A water barrel, for example, will look fine in a corner of the garden, but if it were transposed to centre stage it would seem out of place. An informal collection of different types of container, perhaps including a water barrel, would be a more suitable alternative.

Larger containers, such as old tanks, make splendid centrepieces to more formal gardens, and they can often set the stylistic tone of the whole garden with their decorative motifs. Others, such as terracotta or earthenware pots, will create a simple but pleasing focus. These containers are rarely waterproof and will need to be lined before they can be used. In colder climates many of the more fragile pots will have to be drained for the winter to avoid frost damage.

A fallen, terracotta pot pours water over loose cobbles. The water sinks to an underground reservoir before being recirculated by a submersible pump.

Containers can be drilled and tipped at an angle to allow water to be piped through them, and this creates an ideal source of water for use at the side of a pool or above a small basin used to catch the falling water. A bubble fountain within a pot will produce a boiling or simmering effect with water brimming over the rim and spilling down over the sides possibly onto paving or pebbles below. This system relies on the use of an underground reservoir (see Chapters 4 and 5). A hole for the necessary pipework from below needs to be waterproofed with either a suitable sealant or with a mechanical seal.

Almost any kind of container can be adapted for the storage of water, from watering cans to lavatories, from buckets to basins, and the resulting effects can be highly decorative or just plain amusing. Many can be both functional and decorative, and the potential of these features in garden design should not be underestimated. They are relatively low in cost and in maintenance but potentially high in impact. Architectural salvage yards and auction houses provide a source of suitable containers, although prices can often be inflated.

BUILT-IN CONTAINERS

Built-in, raised containers over 1m (3ft 3in) in height should be constructed in a similar way to retaining walls because, depending on size, the water can exert considerable pressure on the retaining structure. For structures below this height, use a two brick thick wall 215mm (8¼in) to provide the necessary strength. A single brick thickness is insufficient. Concrete block or in-situ concrete may be used, but this will probably need a decorative facing material to improve its appearance.

Flexible liners may be used in these rigid structures, and they can be tailored to the exact dimensions of the pool. However, it is also possible to obtain prefabricated waterproof tanks, and some manufacturers will make tanks to your own specifications in glass reinforced plastic or PVC.

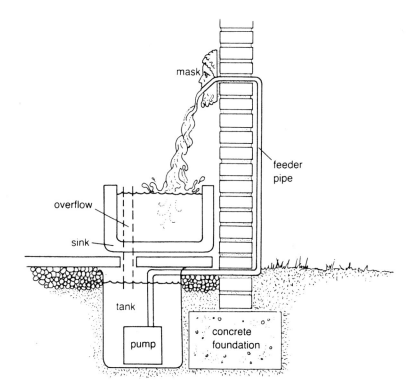

Wall masks are popular features, but they require careful planning to minimize the impact of the necessary pipework. If the mask is mounted on a free-standing wall the pipes can be routed on the back face of the wall and perhaps disguised by planting. On a party or boundary wall this will not be possible, and the pipes will have to be recessed into the surface of the wall. A simple stone sink makes an ideal receptacle for the spout of water, although pots, urns and tanks are equally decorative.

A simple but effective way of creating a water feature is to use a prefabricated tank. These are available in various kinds of plastic or in glass reinforced plastic (grp), and they can either be dropped into a recess in the ground or contained within walls. If you use walls, coping will be needed to disguise the awkward junction or gap between the walls and the tank.

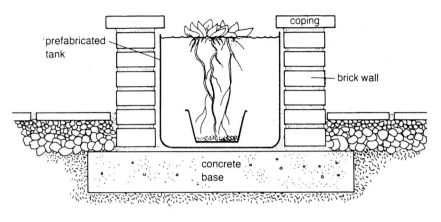

These features work well when they are combined with an existing wall or structure, and spouts or wall-mounted masks dropping water from above can be introduced for movement and decorative effect. Simple garden taps may also be treated in this way, with containers introduced beneath decorative fittings to provide an incidental feature.

chapter seven

SCULPTURAL *and* ORNAMENTAL FEATURES

Water alone is a fascinating medium to use in the garden, challenging both to manipulate and to control. Many artists have been drawn to this challenge, and the work of sculptors and three-dimensional designers is often associated with water in some form. Water may be part of a sculptural work, or the two elements may stand separately for reflective and contemplative effect, and the strong link between artificial sculpted forms and the softness of water in the landscape or garden setting is irresistible. The decorative ornamentation and embellishment of water, although not as closely linked, may also provide a rich source of visual interest and stimulation. The permutations of suitable shapes, forms, materials, and styles in ornament or sculpture make this area of water garden design most appealing to the adventurous.

SCULPTURE

Sculpture is an artistic exploration of three-dimensional form, sometimes using mass and weight, sometimes exploiting transparency and delicacy. Of the twentieth-century sculptors, Henry Moore typifies the former both with his figurative and abstract work, while the spindle-thin figures of Alberto Giacommetti typify the latter. Geoffrey Jellicoe used Ben Nicholson's white marble bas-relief wall at Sutton Place, Surrey, to create a sensational combination of water and sculpture, providing vivid reflections in a dark, mirror-smooth pool. Other artists specialize in transparent materials, such as glass or perspex, some with solid stone and heavy metal, while one or two play with the qualities of water itself.

In early spring, the moss covered banks of this mill-race are decorated by Narcissus *flowers. The sleepy stone lion fits perfectly into this atmospheric scene.*

Whatever the medium used, the sculptures themselves may be seen as passive objects, associated with, or used alongside, water for direct contrast, and the manipulation and creation of reflections as part of the overall effect is an important aspect of the design. Alternatively, the sculptural forms may interact with, and perhaps also control the flow or movement of, water. Kinetic sculptures work in this way, with moving jets or streams of water

This bathing figure draws attention to the water, inviting exploration and discovery.

striking parts of the sculpture, which then move or collide to create new arrangements or sounds.

In figurative work the sculpted forms may be associated with water, and fish or sea creatures are common. Human figures emerging through the surface of a pool or spouting water are equally popular, perhaps influenced by the writhing baroque or renaissance forms of fable and mythology seen in so many great gardens. The Bassin d'Apollon and the Bassin de Neptune at Versailles typify this use of figurative statuary, which, in their original positions, created a tumultous mass of fabulous figures emerging from the watery depths.

The simplicity and grace of contemporary figurative sculptures are often more effective and evocative, or the sculptors use modern engineering principles to create seemingly impossible states of equilibrium. In abstract work the sculpted forms may explore geometric, textural, colourful or three-dimensional ideas. The contrasts in shape or form, surface treatment or colour are essential to the success of these forms, and the qualities of water as a passive or dynamic element often play a role in their success. The effect and impact of light on these forms is also an important consideration as are the changing atmospheric conditions.

Of prime importance, however, are the positioning and framing of the sculpture in question. If a water feature and sculptural work can be considered together as a single concept from the outset of planning or redesigning a garden the greater the chances of a successful design solution. It is extremely difficult to introduce sculpture into a location at random or at whim. Sometimes, the two elements may combine completely to produce

OPPOSITE Sculpture can work successfully in a waterside setting. This slender figure by Marzia Colonna contrasts elegantly with the textures of the planting and the reflective pool.

land sculpture or land art in which the ground or the water feature may create sculptural impact, and here the complexities of three-dimensional design may be explored to the full.

In contrast, the use of sculptural relief or three-dimensional mural work introduces the possibilities of vibrant colour in the form of ceramics and mosaic. This may be used in association with water, either to exploit the reflective qualities of the surface or to refresh the qualities of such surfaces seen through clear water.

Darkening the base of a pool gives the strongest reflections and allows the water surface to act like a mirror so that any sense of detail or depth is lost. If the pool base is treated with a much brighter colour, surface reflections are almost negligible and the base colour shines through the depth of water, an effect most easily observed in swimming pools. Any pattern or design included in such a treatment may either be viewed through perfectly still water or may be activated, as in a painting by David Hockney, by disturbing the water surface, so that the waves or ripples disjoint the pattern to sensational effect.

Japanese garden designers utilize a similar effect by laying pebbles in decorative patterns on the base of their shallow pools and streams. A combination of pebbles of different sizes or colours is used to line a pool, and when the water surface is disturbed, perhaps by a spray or sprinkler, a myriad of patterns is produced.

OPPOSITE *A startling sculpture for a startling garden. In the jungle-like atmosphere created by Myles Challis, a giant hand emerges from a shadowy pool.*

The clear simplicity of this garden, designed by Thomas Church, is enhanced by the reclining figure, apparently contemplating the tranquility of the pool.

ORNAMENT

Ornamentation within the garden can be wide and diverse, with the majority of artefacts capable of use with water. Pots and containers have already been discussed, but the containment of water is only one aspect of the association between ornament and water.

Obelisks were favourite features in the ancient Mediterranean gardens, but in the seventeenth century André Le Nôtre used them with water cascading down from the pinnacle. Pots, statuary and urns of every description have since undergone this transformation, and the results can be very pleasing. Dull surfaces are seen to sparkle with movement and light, and algal growth can add to the patina in a most decorative way. Copper, lead and bronze produce particularly strong and exaggerated results with the rivulets of water staining and marking in colourful and interesting patterns.

Wall-mounted plaques may be used as a decorative source of water, either with a built-in basin or spouting into a separate collecting pot. Individual bowls or basins can also be arranged to catch flowing water, forming a wall-mounted cascade. On a more simple or functional level an ornamental garden tap can become a decorative feature with a collecting dish or container beneath to catch the drips. Cascades, fountains, jets and reflective pools have all been tried and tested, but fine mist spray nozzles surrounding these artefacts can produce mysterious and ethereal effects that are well worth trying.

The most important consideration when choosing ornament or sculpture for the garden is to find the right scale. There is no definitive guideline, but mistakes are often made in choosing objects that are far too small. We usually measure by the interior spaces with which we are more familiar, but if an object would look appropriate in your living-room, it will almost certainly be insignificant in the garden. The exception to this rule would be in an exterior space that was purposely reduced and intimate in scale, such as a private seating area or in a small town garden.

Ornamental or sculptural work may be classical or contemporary in character, and it may be appropriate to a variety of situations. There is no golden rule of application, and contemporary works can produce stunning contrasts with period settings, while decorative garden antiques will not look out of place in a modern location. These counterpoints are fun to experiment with, and there is something deeply satisfying in matching these opposites. Some might feel a certain trepidation, in which case harmonizing these forms or matching styles would prove more satisfactory. Water in association with these ideas often brings further excitement and emphasis. For complex and specialist water sculpture, it is best to allow the artist responsible for the work or the garden designer to install or to construct.

chapter eight

LIGHTING

The quality of light is essential to the success of water in the garden. In our mind's eye we probably imagine or develop a picture of a sparkling cascade in bright daylight or sunlit reflections glowing with warmth and brilliance. Yet in the evenings, when darkness falls and these qualities are lost, water can take on dangerous and disquieting dimensions. The liveliness of water and its value within the garden need not end with the sunset, however, as artificial light can prolong and redefine our perceptions. Modern technology has miniaturized and improved light fittings to make almost any effect or desire possible.

It is important that all electrical fixtures and fittings are as invisible by day as they are by night. The magic produced by clever lighting needs careful consideration, planning and implementation. Some light fittings are designed to be seen, and these may be relatively easily placed for safety, security or decorative purposes. Lighting in association with water will almost certainly be included for purely decorative reasons, and it is the effect or the quality of the light that is important, rather than the appearance of the light fitting itself. This emphasis will mean that where possible the fitting should be hidden from view, or cowled in some way to reduce the impact of the light source.

To achieve the best effect when using lighting with water, the water must be filtered and maintained for absolute clarity, otherwise its murky quality will be accentuated. If water is to be lit from within then the light source should sit on the viewer's side of the pool, thus being out of sight, allowing a general glow of light under water with a highlighting of the furthest bank. Lighting placed into a pool of water would illuminate the liner, wiring or pump mechanism and the planting around the pool might appear only in silhouette.

Alternatively, the water may be left as a dark mass while the surrounding landscape is defined with light. This will produce strong and shimmering reflections, as the same principle applies to the painting of a pool in a dark colour to improve reflective quality. Pools for recreational use, such as

Here the backdrop to a small garden pool has been floodlit, a technique which enhances reflections on the water surface.

99

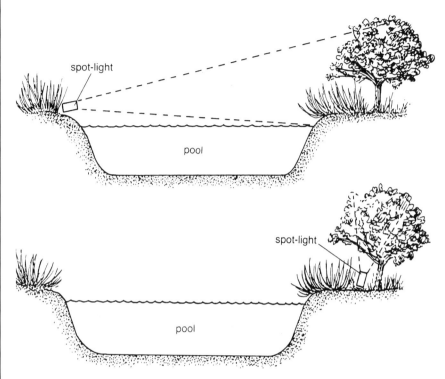

Positioning lights on one bank to shine across to the other side to highlight features there or using up-lights or spot-lights below or next to a feature is often more successful than trying to introduce lighting into a body of water. Not only must the water be clear, the pumps, pipework and cabling may be difficult to disguise.

swimming pools or jacuzzis, work well with underwater lighting because they also have in-built filtration systems to keep the water clear and clean. A purely decorative pool will generally appear murky and opaque by comparison and will not, therefore, be shown to best advantage. This lighting is an expensive option as the necessary safety requirements increase the cost.

The most successful effects are achieved by using white light, provided by a low-voltage halogen bulb, or a soft yellow tint, produced by tungsten and pale green, emitted by mercury, which works well with planting. Sufficient colour will be picked out to make the night scene attractive and interesting. Green, red or blue light, or a combination of all three, will introduce unexpected qualities into the garden, with flower or foliage colour registering as black or grey, neither of which are particularly flattering. These effects can be quite surreal and should be carefully considered before their introduction.

One way of avoiding startling or direct light, is to light from a distance, perhaps from a nearby tree canopy or structure. This softer glow of light can enhance the waterside scene and will work effectively from the house. In any case, the intensity or brightness of lighting or at least lighting effects needs to vary, even in the smallest scheme. This technique maintains a level of visual interest which is generally appealing. Bright lighting effects throughout the garden will reduce the quality of shadow and will render

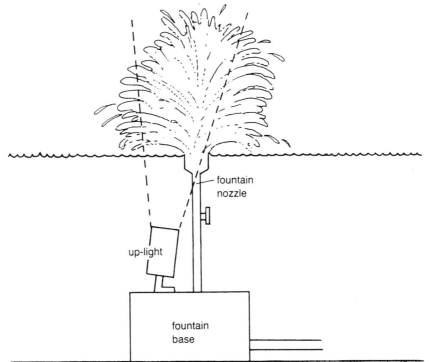

If lighting is included within the water, try to line up the elements as closely as possible. An up-light placed directly under a fountain will light it rather than the water in general.

fountain nozzle

up-light

fountain base

most features flat, and a lighting level that is too low will lose sharpness and focus and render the lighting scheme almost worthless.

Individual features, such as fountains, cascades and sculpture, will be improved at night with well-aimed spotlights, either mounted at some distance or, more dramatically, at the base of the feature. Additionally, a number of spot-lights may be used to emit light from different directions, and this can increase the sense of movement in the water and add depth. Dropping lighting units into the ground to provide a vertical shaft of light from below is particularly effective for enhancing form and texture, and it works well below tree canopies. The qualities of branching patterns are enhanced by this technique, making lighting effective for winter use. In summer, additional fixtures may be necessary to illuminate the same tree, because the foliage will greatly reduce light penetration into the canopy. The light sources may be contained within the canopy itself or mounted at some distance to provide an overall glow. Placing the fixtures high in a tree canopy makes possible an effect known as moonlighting, and when a soft, white light is used, the glow from high above the garden simulates the soft, silvery light of the moon filtering through the branches.

Sculptures and ornamental features used in association with water can prove particularly effective when they are lit. It is important to get the best out of such features, and the placing of individual spotlights should be carefully considered. In general, it is best to light three-dimensional forms or

101

reliefs from an angle, perhaps from the side or from below so that the shadows cast by the surface features or patterns become part of the decorative effect and contrast with the highlighted features.

Lighting systems no longer need to be static displays. Many spot-lights are now available fitted with spikes and extension cables, so that they can be placed in alternative positions. These systems are worth considering, especially in newly planted gardens, where the light fixtures can be moved as the planting matures.

Lasers and fibres optics are also available for exciting and dynamic effects. Lasers can be targeted to point up a particular feature or they can track across the sky, while fibre optics can be combined with planting to produce an unusual, soft glow. This is best used for less accessible areas, because the cables and wires are often visible in daylight. A variety of colour combinations is possible with these facilities, and the final choice will be a matter of personal taste.

Lighting extends the use of the garden, both visually and functionally, once darkness has fallen. Here lights have been used within the pool, an effect that relies on the cleanliness of the water and on cables or pipes within the feature.

PRACTICAL CONSIDERATIONS

It is best to locate any necessary switches for electrical works within the house, and it is essential that any outdoor wiring is fitted with a circuit breaker for reasons of safety. When siting the cable, steer clear of any areas that are regularly cultivated. The cable running into the garden must be protected or armoured and should run 60cm (2ft) below ground level; you should also keep a record of the route and mark it.

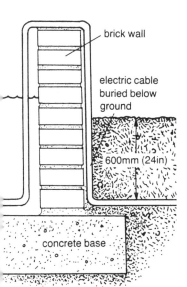

brick wall

electric cable buried below ground

600mm (24in)

concrete base

The introduction of low-voltage systems has made the use of lighting in the garden much safer. Nevertheless, cable routes should be carefully recorded and should avoid areas that are subject to a lot of traffic or regular cultivation. A depth of 600mm (24in) below ground level is recommended, and the electric cable should run in a protective conduit.

Low-voltage lighting requires a transformer, which is best located within the house. If it has to be sited outside, a weatherproof structure or casing is required. The fittings themselves are small and discreet, installation is simple, and there is much less danger. The cables do not need to be buried deep in the ground, and they can be fixed to fences or walls. However, for considerations of safety, if the cable is to be buried, it is good practice to contain the run within a conduit, to mark the route and keep a record of it. Over any lengthy run of cable there will be a voltage loss or reduction, and the maximum working distance is 30m (100ft). This can mean that the positioning of the transformer within the house is not workable if a pool is located at the end of a long garden. For distances greater than 30m (100ft), either a 240 volt system should be used or a 240 volt cable should run to a centrally placed transformer.

The voltage drop is influenced by distance or length of cable, by the number of fittings included in the design and by the conductor size of cable. In any system, the acceptable voltage loss is 5 per cent, and so for a 12 volt system the maximum allowable voltage drop will be 0.6 volt. Transformers for low-voltage systems should be matched in size to within 10 per cent of the operating load. If the transformer is to be situated in the garden the housing should be raised above ground level by at least 75mm (3in), preferably on a wall or other vertical surface. This may make disguise difficult, and suitable locations should be considered carefully.

The installation costs of low-voltage systems are much lower than the 240 volt counterpart, partly because of the lower cost of fixtures but also because of the reduced labour costs of installation. The units are also energy efficient. A 50 watt 12 volt lamp can provide the same amount of light as a 150 watt incandescent fixture. The more lighting combinations required, the more complex the wiring, although it is possible to create a circuit from which a number of lighting units feed. For anything more than a basic system it is advisable to consult a specialist in outdoor electrics.

For underwater lighting it may be necessary to use weights to keep the fittings in place. In addition, it is good practice to allow an amount of slack cable in case of future movement. Most fittings are supplied with cables ready attached, which means that any necessary junctions can be made on dry land. Underwater lighting carries with it a higher degree of maintenance, as silt, algal growth and other deposits can cloud the cover and impair light quality.

If you have any queries about the choice or installation of lighting it is best to consult a lighting designer, preferably one who is a specialist in outdoor systems. Additionally, the on-going maintenance should be considered from the outset and thought of as an essential part of the design process. A fitting that produces dramatic results but is difficult to access will not prove effective in the long term.

chapter nine

PLANTING *in* and around WATER

Although water may be used as a decorative element in its own right, the enhancing effects of plant material are well worth considering and, in the case of aquatic species, may be essential to the habitat that is created. Water planting allows a wide range of foliage textures and flower shapes to be introduced to the garden.

This chapter describes some of the plants that can be grown in and around water. This covers a wide range of material, some of which will hardly be noticed, such as the oxygenators that lurk in the depths but bring life and shelter into the pool. Other species, such as the marginals, blow their trumpets of foliage and flower quite unashamedly and provide displays of colour and texture which few other plants in the garden can match.

PLANTING IN WATER

Each distinct group of plants has something to offer in water garden design. Visually, however, it is the plant material that emerges in some way from the water that has the greatest impact on us. This direct relationship with water produces the strongest reflections and the greatest sense of drama. Water replaces the soil here as the main element surrounding the plant material. So instead of a dull backdrop, the plant material is surrounded by a light, reflective and mobile surface. In close detail, water features as planting beds become full of life, vibrant

The tall stems and leaves of iris and rush echo the vertical cascade of clear water, which is also reflected in the spikes of lupin and Digitalis in the borders.

with movement and changing patterns. Individual foliage textures, shapes and forms can be combined, compared and contrasted to great effect.

From a distance the picture of a planted water feature is quite different. Large masses of foliage texture or flower colour may be used to mark the position of water within the garden, but the water itself is often obscured as a result. An expanse of clear water, particularly a feature of any size, will often be evident in the landscape as a sparkling strip of light. Once planted, the reflective surface of water is often hidden from view. While this may introduce an element of surprise in the garden, the overall effect of water is lost.

By planting marginals and emergents in bold, simple groups the presence of water in the garden is announced by definite changes in texture. Few traditional border plants can compete with the bold spear-shapes of reed or iris foliage, and water lilies create floating islands that are impossible to recreate elsewhere. The design qualities of aquatic and marginal plants are often more exaggerated than other plant species and this quality will suit simple and spartan associations in particular. The adage 'less is more' applies particularly in this environment and the arrangement of strong textures, a splash of colour and bold form against the simple beauty of water is difficult to beat.

PLANTING AROUND WATER

There is a wide range of species that prove successful in association with water. Many of these plants may actually prefer wet or damp conditions, while others

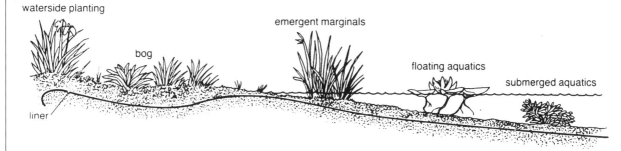

waterside planting

bog

emergent marginals

floating aquatics

submerged aquatics

liner

These different types or areas of planting associated with water are easily achieved with flexible liners.

have no physical inclination for wetter conditions but might simply have something decorative to offer to the waterside environment.

It is important at this planning stage to discriminate between natural and artificial water features, because this basic difference is essential to planting success. If you are lucky enough to own a natural pool or part of a water course, it may be evident that the areas immediately adjacent to the water are different in character from the rest of the garden. In general, there is a greater chance of water-logging, dampness or bogginess, which will be difficult to eradicate. The level of the water table may fluctuate or the area may be prone to flooding. These areas will have overriding damp conditions which are best accepted and catered for in the planting design by creating a bog garden.

Conversely, artificial features are imposed on the landscape. They have nothing to do with natural drainage and there is absolutely no reason to assume that the banks or poolside environment will be damper or wetter than any other part of the garden. This may seem obvious, but the mistake of planting wetland species in dry borders is frequently made.

The art of the water garden designer is to combine either all the various species together or to zone the correct species into the correct environment. A wild water garden will include a number of these different zones. Various habitats such as aquatic, emergent, marginal, bog and dry will be related in a progression from pool depths to dry land. In a more ornamental design this progression may be lost in favour of decorative associations which link different species for colour or textural effects.

The following list of plants is by no means exhaustive and may be extended further with individual and personal choices. The plants are chosen primarily for their decorative merits but their preference for particular conditions is noted.

OXYGENATING PLANTS

The pools and slow-moving stream features discussed earlier are most likely to be used for planting. The lack of circulating and refreshing water in these systems can lead to stagnation. The introduction of plant material in the form of the oxygenating species, which produce and expel oxygen as part of their growth cycle, brings life to the system.

Although these plants are essential, many of them hide their light and once established are often hard to detect. Others decorate the water surface with floating foliage and flowers, and while the reflective surface of a pond may be lost, the ornamental display is some compensation. Many of these seemingly innocent plants are actually extremely vigorous growers and will increase tremendously in bulk over the growing season. It is important to be aware of this propensity before purchase or planting, as the balance of the pool system may easily be lost. Management on some scale is necessary each year to maintain this balance, and the plant material should not be allowed to occupy more than one-third of the overall volume of the water feature.

Callitriche palustris (water starwort)

A hardy submerged aquatic with pale, star-shaped foliage that remains for the most part out of sight. The main growth period of this plant is early spring, while *C. hermaphroditica* will grow over the winter months. The plant will tolerate a range of depths and its spread will need checking.

Ceratophyllum demersum (hornwort)

This is a hardy floating aquatic with long, spreading growth which breaks off easily and starts to root and grow. The foliage is dark green and prefers good light conditions in relatively deep water.

Crassula helmsii

As an evergreen aquatic, this plant is ready to grow given the right conditions. Oxygenation starts early in the spring with a flush of growth.

Eleocharis acicularis (hair grass/needle spike rush)

The fine grass-like leaves of this hardy, evergreen plant are mid-green and produce dense underwater cover in pools up to about 30cm (12in) deep.

Elodea canadensis (Canadian pondweed)

The fast growth of this hardy, evergreen aquatic can be overwhelming, and it needs to be controlled. It will either root at some depth or float freely in the water. Fish feed on this plant and use its cover for spawning. This plant is not suitable for smaller pools.

Lagarosiphon major (curly water thyme)

This is hardy, evergreen and one of the best oxygenators. It grows in a similar way to *Elodea*. The stems are covered in narrow, dark green leaves. It is often sold under the name *Elodea crispa*.

Lemna minor (common duckweed)

Duckweed is common in natural ponds and much favoured by fish. It is hardy and can grow rapidly and quickly gets out of hand. A much lesss rampant alternative is *L. trisulca* (ivy-leaved duckweed).

Myriophyllum verticillatum (whorled water milfoil)

The stems of this hardy plant bear finely dissected, bright green foliage, which fish utilize for spawning. M. *aquaticum*, the parrot's feather, is tender and is controlled by reduced temperature, although it is rarely killed off completely.

Potamogeton crispus (curled pondweed)

The wavy, seaweed-like foliage of this hardy aquatic has a bronze hue which colours more vividly in strong light conditions.

Ranunculus aquatilis (water crowfoot)

This hardy plant is probably one of the most attractive oxygenators. It has dissected foliage below the water line and three-lobed, floating leaves, which are decorated in the spring with tiny white flowers.

SUBMERGED AND FLOATING AQUATIC PLANTS

This is a range of plants with root systems that penetrate the depths of pools or ditches but that produce displays of foliage and flower at or above the water surface. Water lilies typify the group and decorate the surface of still water to good effect with their pads and blooms. The flat leaves of these plants emphasize the horizontal plane of the water surface, and they also work well in association with the more vertical marginal or emergent plants, which will be discussed later.

These plants prefer still water, although they will tolerate slow-moving currents. However, the root systems can hamper water movement and encourage silting processes if they become extremely dense. It is useful to plant the more vigorous species into wire baskets, which can then be immersed. However, this solution is not infallible and plant material will still

Pools made of hard materials will require planting shelves to accommodate the different types of planting at the necessary depths of water.

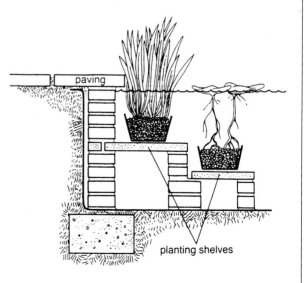

107

spread or root outside the barrier provided by the cage, so it is essential to check plants regularly for excessive growth.

In addition, it is useful to note the various depths of planting, because this will promote successful establishment and stronger growth. Many designers will plant into soil pockets placed directly on the liner, and the contouring of the excavation can accommodate recesses or shelves for this purpose. In larger water features this is the best method of planting in any case, because baskets would be uneconomical. The depth of water can also frequently act as a restricting factor on plant colonization.

Aponogeton distachyos (water hawthorn)

The strongly scented white flowers of this hardy plant are often produced throughout the year. They are accompanied by long, strap-shaped floating leaves, which decorate the water surface. Plant at a depth of 15cm (6in) deep and later move to 30–45cm (12–18in) as the plant becomes established.

Hottonia palustris (water violet)

This hardy floating plant is particularly useful for shallower pools and provides a display of delicate pale mauve flowers above the water level in spring and summer. The fern-like, pale green leaves remain under water.

Hydrocharis morsus-ranae (frogbit)

The decorative qualities of this plant are on a small scale, with tiny, round, floating leaves and white flowers produced in summer. The plant floats during the growing season, dropping overwintering buds to the bottom of the pool in winter. The buds rise to the surface in summer when new growth begins.

Nuphar (common yellow water lily)

These water lilies are extremely hardy and will survive quite severe frost. They enjoy deep water and will tolerate shade and slow currents. They will often thrive where other more delicate water lilies fail. Their planting and growth depth is between 1–2m (3ft–6ft 6in) N. lutea, the most common species, provides scented yellow flowers amidst large leaves,

30cm (12in) across. N. advena has more spherical flowers and is available with cream flowers and variegated foliage (N. advena 'Variegata'). N. japonica has more pointed leaves and N. j. var. rubrotinctum has orange flowers.

Nymphaea (water lily)

The water lily is probably the most sought after aquatic plant, and it is certainly one of the most spectacular. Its decorative worth is evidenced by the wide range of varieties and hybrids now available. This is the rose of the water garden, and almost any colour is possible in double and single flower. The planting depths and rates of growth vary tremendously. Those described here are all hardy.

N. alba is the most common European species and one of the most beautiful, with its pure white, cup-shaped flowers and green leaves. They are rampant growers, and thus not suitable for the smaller garden ponds. The individual plant may spread to 2.5m (8ft), and they will grow in depths of 1m (3ft 3in).

N. candida produces white flowers but this plant will spread to 75cm (2ft 6in). The flowers are carried above the water surface. The required depth is approximately 30cm (12in).

The flat pads of Nymphaea *decorate the surface of this reflecting pool. The vertical emphasis of the marginal planting of* Pontederia *provides the essential contrast.*

N. odorata is also white-flowered and prefers shallow water with room to spread to approximately 1.8m (6ft). The planting depth is 30–60cm (1–2ft).

N. tetragona is a small white variety. This lily will spread to 45cm (1ft 6in) and needs water 60–90cm (16in–3ft) deep.

A wide range of hybrids and cultivars is available, mainly distinguished by colour.

Red: *N.* 'Laydekeri' (spread 1m/3ft 3in, depth 25cm/10in), *N.* 'Laydekeri Purpurata' (spread 60–90cm/2–3ft, depth 25cm/10in), *N.* 'Atropurpurea' (spread 1.5m/5ft, depth 60cm/2ft), *N.* 'Attraction' (spread 2.5m/8ft, depth 1m/3ft 3in), *N.* 'Conqueror' (spread 2m/6ft 6in, depth 60cm/2ft), *N.* 'Escarboucle' (spread 2m/6ft 6in, depth 60cm/2ft), *N.* 'Froebelii' (spread 1m/3ft 3in, depth 25cm/10in), *N.* 'Gloriosa' (spread 1.2m/4ft, depth 45cm 1ft 6in), *N.* 'James Brydon' (spread 1.2m/4ft, depth 45cm/ 1ft 6in).

Pink: *N.* × 'Laydekeri Lilacea' (spread 60cm/2ft, depth 30cm/1ft), *N.* 'Marliacea Rosea' (spread 2m/6ft 6in, depth 75cm/2ft 6in), *N.* 'Amabilis' (spread 2m/6ft 6in, depth 75cm/2ft 6in), *N.* 'Helen Fowler' (spread 1.2m/4ft, depth 45cm/1ft 6in), *N.* 'Lustrous' (spread 1.2m/4ft, depth 45cm/1ft 6in), *N.* 'Mary Patricia' (spread 1m/3ft 3in, depth 30–40cm/ 12–16in), *N.* 'Mme. Wilfron Gonnère' (double flower, spread 1.5m/5ft, depth 60cm/2ft), *N.* 'Pink Opal' (spread 1m/3ft 3in, depth 45cm/1ft 6in), *N.* 'Pink Sensation' (spread 1.5m/5ft, depth 45cm/1ft 6in).

White: *N.* 'Marliacea Albida' (spread 2m/6ft 6in, depth 60cm/2ft), *N.* 'Albatros' (spread 1.2m/4ft, depth 45cm/1ft 6in), *N.* 'Gonnère' (spread 1.5m/5ft, depth 60cm/2ft), *N.* 'Hal Miller', cream (spread 1.5m/5ft, depth 60cm/2ft), *N.* 'Hermine' (spread 1m/3ft 3in, depth 30cm/1ft), *N.* 'Virginalis' (spread 2m/6ft 6in, depth 60cm/2ft)

Yellow: *N.* 'Marliacea Chromatella' (spread 2m/ 6ft 6in, depth 75cm/2ft 6in), *N.* 'Aurora' (spread 60cm/2ft, depth 60cm/2ft), *N.* 'Colonel A. J. Welch' (spread 2.8m/9ft, depth 75cm/2ft 6in), *N.* × *helvola* (spread 40cm/16in, depth 25cm/10in), *N.* 'Moorei' (spread 1.5m/5ft, depth 60cm/2ft), *N.* 'Sunrise' (spread 1.5m/5ft, depth 60cm/2ft).

Orontium aquaticum (golden club)
The white, poker-like flowers of *Orontium* are tipped with bright yellow and held high above the dark green foliage. The leaves are silvered beneath and catch reflected light. This hardy plant prefers full sun and a planting depth up to 30cm (12in). Preferably, the initial planting should be in shallower water.

Stratiotes aloides (water soldier)
The olive green leaf rosettes of the water soldier float just under the surface until flowering time, when it rises to the surface. Cup-shaped white flowers are produced in summer. This hardy plant is also a useful oxygenator and it prefers alkaline water and good sun.

Utricularia vulgaris (bladderwort)
This is an unusual plant for the garden as it is carnivorous. The leaves have small bladders that catch tiny creatures floating in the water. The vivid yellow flowers are the most decorative feature held above the water. Although tender, the bladderwort will spread widely.

EMERGENT AND MARGINAL PLANTS

Many aqautic plants flower at, or just above, water level with most of the plant hidden below. However, there is also a wide range of species that have their roots in water and their foliage and flower above. Such species provide the essential vertical contrast to the horizontal plane of the water surface and the flat leaves of the aquatics. These contrasts are strong and direct, a feast for the designer and exciting to manipulate. It is tempting to overuse them, but the strength of these planting associations lies in the ability to exercise restraint and be selective.

Flower form and colour, foliage texture and shape, plant size and the stem structure all provide the means for contrasts and harmonies to be exploited, just as in the typical garden border. The major difference here is that water plants tend to exaggerate these characteristics, producing extremes in design combinations.

In the excitement of the planting process the qualities of the water feature itself should not be overlooked or ignored. Utilize the reflective passivity

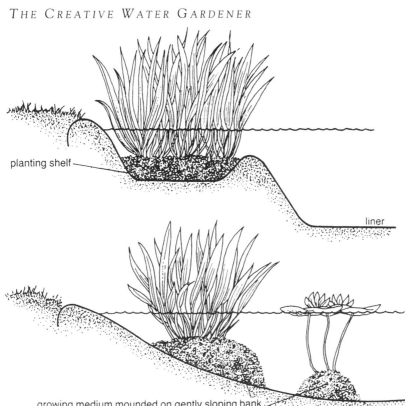

planting shelf

liner

growing medium mounded on gently sloping bank

Where possible, plant aquatic subjects directly in the soil, which can be mounded on the liner in the required positions. Although the soil is often blinded with gravel or pebbles to protect the plant roots and restrict soil movement, this is not usually necessary, especially where water disturbance is kept to a minimum. Planting shelves, contoured into the bank profiles, are generally the most satisfactory solution, and the soil can be retained by the shaping of the ground under the liner. In rigid pools planting baskets are an alternative.

of the water surface to balance the drama of planting textures. Allow the neutral backdrop of deep water to counteract the flower colours and allow each material to speak. In addition, if the overall shape of the feature is strong or important then this must not be lost, at least not in total. Allow hard edges or bank treatments to contrast with the plant material just as in any other part of the garden.

Acorus calamus (sweet flag)

The sword shaped spiky leaves of *Acorus* are similar to iris but will exude a sweet fruity scent when crushed or bruised. The flowers are not significant. It is a hardy, semi-evergreen perennial. Height 60cm (2ft), planting depth 15–30cm (6–12in). *A. calamus* 'Variegatus' is a variegated form with cream stripes to the leaf.

Acorus gramineus (Japanese rush)

This hardy plant is a smaller version of *A. calamus*, forming a low clump of dark green spiky foliage. Height 30cm (12in), planting depth 10–15cm (4–6in). *A. gramineus* 'Variegatus' is the cream variegated form. *A.g.* 'Ogon' has gold banding.

Alisma plantago-aquatica (great water plantain)

This is a hardy, deciduous perennial. The flowers are of most interest, with pyramidal lilac heads growing up to 60cm (2ft) high. The leaves are upright and bright green. They will self seed very easily and may need to be controlled. Height 60cm (2ft), planting depth 10–15cm (4–6in).

Butomus umbellatus (flowering rush)

The flowering rush is a hardy, deciduous perennial. It combines spectacular flower with strong foliage texture. The pink flowers are produced in summer, with umbels carried high above the spiked foliage. Height 1m (3ft 3in), planting depth 10–12 cm (4–4¾in).

Calla palustris (bog arum)

This perennial plant enjoys the wet soil that is found right on the water's edge, producing white arum-like spathes in spring which are followed by dramatic spikes of orange-red fruits in the late summer or autumn. The broad, glossy foliage forms an excellent pool edge plant. Height 25cm (10in), planting depth to 10cm (4in).

Caltha palustris (marsh marigold, kingcup)
This is a hardy, deciduous or semi-evergreen plant. The sunshine yellow flowers make it one of the most popular species in the water garden. The flowers come early in the season and are set against rich dark green foliage. This plant also does well in bog conditions. Height 30–40cm (12–16in), planting depth up to 10cm (4in). There is also a double-flowered form, C. palustris 'Flore Pleno'.

Eriophorum angustifolium (common cotton grass)
This hardy, fine-leaved grass produces attractive white seedheads with a soft texture. Often seen in the wild, this grass enjoys damp and wet soils. Height 30cm (1ft), planting depth up to 5cm (2in).

Glyceria maxima var. variegata (reed sweet grass)
The rampant and rapid growth of this pale yellow variegated grass needs careful consideration before planting. It is a hardy, herbaceous grass. If included in smaller water features then container or basket planting is advised. Height 60cm (2ft), planting depth approximately 10cm (4in).

Houttuynia cordata
The blue-green leaves and red-brown stems of this hardy, deciduous perennial make interesting colour contrasts. The form 'Chameleon' produces leaves splashed with red and yellow for a more vivid display best seen in full sun. The leaves are orange-scented when crushed. Height to 30cm (1ft), planting depth to 10cm (4in). This plant can be quite invasive.

Iris ensata syn. **I. kaempferi** (Japanese flag)
This iris is one of the most beautiful plants and is suitable for marginal planting along the very edge of the water or in boggy conditions. The purple or red-purple flowers are mass produced in early summer with many garden forms offering a wide range of variations in colour and pattern. Some shade is preferred in acid conditions. Drier winter soils preferred. It is a hardy perennial. Height 60cm–1m (2–3ft 3in), planting depth up to 3cm (1¼in).

The delicate vertical tracery of rushes and other marginals such as iris provides important accents in water planting.

Iris laevigata
The blue or white flowers of this iris are marked with yellow to provide strong colour in late spring or early summer. Wet or boggy conditions are preferred in sun or dappled shade. It is a hardy perennial. Height 60cm–1m (2–3ft 3in), planting depth up to 10cm (4in). 'Colchesterensis' has large white flowers, 'Regal' carries pink-red flowers and 'Snowdrift', which suits smaller pools, has double white flowers.

Iris pseudacorus (yellow flag)
This plant is a vigorous grower with tall stems of bright yellow flowers carried high above masses of foliage in early to mid summer. It is a hardy perennial, the size of which suits larger pools. Height up to 2m (6ft 6in), planting depth 15–20cm (6–8in). 'Variegata' has yellow striped foliage.

111

The brilliant yellow spathes of Lysichiton americanus *decorate the water margins in spring, before the majority of plants are in leaf.*

Juncus effusus (soft rush)
This hardy, evergreen species produces slender erect spikes of dark glossy foliage but it is seldom seen in cultivation. More commonly the rather curious variety, *J. effusus* 'Spiralis', the corkscrew rush, is seen, with contorted and spiralling leaves. Height 45cm (1ft 6in), planting depth 10–15cm (4–6in).

Lysichiton americanus (bog arum)
The yellow arum-like spathes of this hardy, deciduous perennial are produced in spring before the leaves which add bold texture to the pool margins. Height 1.5m (5ft), planting depth up to 5cm (2in).

Lysichiton camtschatcensis
This is a hardy, deciduous perennial. Similar in appearance to *L. americanus*, the spathes, carried in spring, are a more attractive pure white. Height 75cm (2ft 6in), planting depth up to 5cm (2in).

Mentha aquatica (water mint)
The finer leaf texture of this hardy, perennial mint works well against the bold foliage of *Lysichiton* or *Iris*. The lilac flowers prove very attractive to bees in the summer. Height 45cm (1ft 6in), planting depth up to 10cm (4in). This plant is invasive.

Menyanthes trifoliata (bog bean)
This marginal produces a carpet of white flowers just above water level in the spring often covering the water's edge and blurring the division between land and water. Mid-green leaves are borne in threes on a single stem. A variety of insects use the plant for food or cover, which is useful for increasing wildlife potential. It is a hardy, deciduous perennial, height 30cm (1ft), planting depth up to 10cm (4in).

Myosotis scorpioides (water forget-me-not)
The tiny blue flowers of this hardy, deciduous perennial produce a cloud of colour over the water surface or in bog conditions in summer. The plant tolerates shade well and seeds easily. Height 20 cm (8in), planting depth up to 10cm (4in).

Ranunculus flammula (lesser spearwort)
This hardy, perennial plant suits smaller pools or containers. It has delicate lemon yellow flowers, produced in early summer, and a lightly branched structure. Height 30cm (1ft), planting depth up to 10cm (4in).

Ranunculus lingua (greater spearwort)
This larger spearwort suits larger pools. Its bright yellow flowers, almost twice the size of the *R. lingua*, are produced in summer. Height 1m (3ft 3in), planting depth 15cm (6in). It is a hardy perennial.

Sagittaria sagittifolia (arrowhead)
The arrow-shaped leaves are the main attraction of this hardy, deciduous perennial, though small white flowers are also produced to decorative effect. Height 45cm (1ft 6in), planting depth 15cm (6in). *S. latifolia* is a more delicate version.

Zantedeschia is one of the most elegant of water garden plants. The clear white spathes are ideally planted alongside reflective water surfaces.

Sparganium erectum (bur reed)

This is a large and vigorous grower producing powerful sword-shaped leaves and decorative, round, greenish-brown flower heads in summer. Restricted growth in a container is recommended. Height to 1.2m (4ft), planting depth 15cm (6in). It is a hardy, deciduous or semi-evergreen perennial.

Typha angustifolia (lesser reedmace)

The common name is deceiving as this is a rampant grower suitable for larger pools and lakes. The grey-green foliage is most attractive and spiked through with brown felted pokers of flower, produced in summer. Control of the growth and spread is essential. Height up to 2m (6ft 6in), planting depth 15–20cm (6–8in). It is a hardy, deciduous perennial.

Typha latifolia (great reedmace)

On an even larger scale to *T. angustifolia*, this is really unsuitable for anything less than a large lake. It has clumps of mid-green foliage and produces spikes of beige flowers in summer. This hardy, deciduous perennial is rampant and invasive with sharp roots which can damage liners. Height up to 3m (10ft), planting depth approximately 15–20cm (6–8in).

Typha minima (miniature reedmace)

This is the only reedmace suitable for the smaller garden pool and is recommended in restricted features, container or basket planting. It has grass-like leaves and rust-brown flowers in late summer. It is a hardy, deciduous perennial. Height 60cm (2ft), planting depth 10cm (4in).

Veronica beccabunga (brooklime)

The creeping habit of this plant is useful to disguise the edge of a pool or water feature. The small blue flowers, produced throughout summer, are contrasted well against the dark leaves. Height 30cm (1ft), planting depth up to 10cm (4in). It is hardy and herbaceous.

Zantedeschia aethiopica (arum lily)

This slightly tender perennial plant is hardy if under water to the required depth. The elegant white spathes, produced in late spring and summer, are certainly worth the effort. Height 1.2m (4ft), planting depth 15–30cm (6–12in), but introduce at a shallower depth initially. 'Crowborough' tends to be tougher once mature and more tolerant of dry periods.

TREES

Trees in association with water produce spectacular effects with the possibility of good reflections and the excitement of dappled light and contrasts of light and shade. Their size and proportions can also help to offset the scale of larger water features, introducing focal points or accents.

Not every garden can take trees, and it is important to consider the scale of the planned water feature and the available space. The mature height and spread of the majority of trees can be dramatic and damaging if they are wrongly used. Thus, the decision to plant must not be taken without research and advice.

The advantages and decorative value of trees should be weighed against leaf drop for deciduous species, for this can produce extra pond maintenance, and the effects of shade and the penetration or disruption of waterproofing systems. The effect of excavation for new water features on existing trees should also be considered. As a rule, the root spread of a given tree will be as extensive as the canopy overhead.

Despite these considerations, trees are of great value and the following suggestions may inspire and guide your choice.

Acer griseum (paper bark maple)

There is a wide variety of maples to choose from, but this is a relatively small tree, with good autumn colour and decorative, peeling, cinnamon-coloured bark. Height, 10m (33ft). Spread, 7cm (23ft). Deciduous, hardy; well-drained.

Alnus glutinosa (common alder)

This tree has a close association with water, thriving in wet or damp conditions. Catkins are produced in the spring and the female flowers remain on the tree as small cones. Height, up to 20m (66ft). Spread, 10m (33ft); suitable for larger features and gardens. Deciduous, hardy; wet.

Arbutus × andrachnoides

The peeling, orange-brown bark of this tree is contrasted well against dark-green foliage. White flowers are produced between autumn and spring, and are followed by strawberry-like fruits. Needs protection from frost when young. Height, 7m (23ft). Spread, 5m (16ft). Evergreen and frost hardy; well-drained.

Betula pendula (silver birch)

The light canopy and delicate hanging foliage of the silver birch allows the white trunk and branches to be revealed. The autumn colour of this tree is normally a clear yellow. Height, 15m (49ft). Spread, 10m (33ft). Deciduous, hardy; well-drained–moist. *B. pendula* 'Laciniata', and 'Youngii' are alternative varieties worth selecting. In addition, *B. utilis* var. *jacquemontii* or *B. papyrifera* may also be considered for their pure white bark.

Catalpa bignonioides (Indian bean tree)

This is a most decorative tree, which produces contorted branching patterns. The leaves are large, and coppicing the tree will produce an even greater leaf size. White flowers are followed by long, elegant pods which hang from the branches well into the winter. Height, 15m (49ft). Spread, 12m (39ft 4in). Deciduous, hardy; well-drained – damp.

Cornus controversa 'Variegata' (wedding cake tree)

The layered branches of this small tree provide the common name. The broad leaves are variegated with cream-white margins. They hang downwards, and the white flower panicles are held erect above and along each branch in late spring. Height, 8m (26ft). Spread, 8m (26ft). Deciduous, hardy; well-drained. The genus *Cornus* includes many shrubs and small trees with coloured stems and branches (see also page 118).

Cupressus cashmeriana (Kashmir cypress)

The weeping, aromatic grey foliage of this large conifer produces a strongly textured blue-green backdrop with a vertical emphasis. This quality contrasts well with water. Height, 15m (49ft). Spread, 10m (33ft). Evergreen; well-drained. This tree is not fully hardy.

Davidia involucrata (dove or handkerchief tree)

The dove tree is most famous for its flowers. These are actually white bracts, which hang down from the branches like handkerchieves. This pendulous effect would suit reflective water features well, although the tree only flowers when it is mature. Height, 12m (39ft 4in). Spread, 8m (26ft). Deciduous; moist but well-drained. Hardy but needs wind protection.

Eucalyptus gunnii (cider gum)

The grey-blue aromatic foliage of the Eucalyptus is a most decorative feature. When young, the trees produce juvenile foliage which is small and circular. This foliage may be retained by coppicing the plant to produce a shrub form. Height, 20m (66ft). Spread, 8m (26ft). Evergreen, frost hardy; well-drained.

Laburnum × watereri 'Vossii' (Voss's laburnum)

The long, bright yellow, pendent flowers are perfect for reflected colour and well worth the short-lived effect in late spring or early summer. Height, 10m (33ft). Spread, 8m (26ft). Deciduous; well-drained – moist. Hardy but best in full sun.

Liquidambar styraciflua (sweet gum)

This well-shaped tree is mainly grown for its brilliant autumn colour in shades of red, orange and burgundy. 'Worplesdon' and 'Lane Roberts' are clones selected for their stunning and reliable autumn colour. Height, 20m (66ft). Spread, 10m (33ft). Deciduous, hardy; moist but well-drained. Shallow chalk soils should be avoided.

Magnolia wilsonii

This Magnolia is particularly useful for association with water. The large, fragrant, white flowers hang down from arching branches in late spring or early summer. This plant may be tender in some areas, preferring a sheltered site with some shade. Height, 7m (23ft). Spread, 7m (23ft). Deciduous, frost hardy; well-drained.

Nyssa sylvatica (tupel)

The elegant branches of this tree glow with strong autumn colour, ranging from yellow and orange to scarlet and purple. Height, 18m (59ft). Spread, 10m (33ft). Deciduous; moist lime-free soil.

115

Prunus × subhirtella 'Autumnalis' (autumn cherry)

This cherry produces delicate white blossoms on bare branches in the autumn and winter months to bring interest to the waterside even in the coldest times of the year. Height, 8m (26ft). Spread, 8m (26ft). Deciduous, hardy; well-drained – moist.

Robinia pseudoacacia 'Frisia' (false acacia)

The feathery leaves of this tree are a bright yellow-green, providing contrast with darker evergreens in particular. Height, 15m (49ft). Spread, 8m (26ft). Deciduous, hardy; well-drained – damp.

Salix alba var. vitellina (golden willow)

This spreading and weeping willow is useful for stem colour. If the branches are pruned or cut back then the orange-yellow bark will provide an excellent display of colour in the winter. S. daphnoides has purple branches while S. alba var. sericea has silver foliage. Height, 15m (49ft). Spread, 10m (33ft). Deciduous, hardy; damp – wet.

Salix × chrysocoma (weeping willow)

This is probably the most famous waterside plant, favoured all over the world for its reflective charm. Space is essential to accommodate this tree to good effect. Height, 18m (59ft). Spread, 20m (66ft). Deciduous, hardy; damp – wet.

Sorbus aria 'Lutescens'

The white felted leaves are particularly intensely coloured in the spring as the buds open, producing a blossom-like effect. The leaves remain a silvery-green before colouring up for autumn. The white flowers of early summer produce clusters of red berries in the autumn. Height, 12m (39ft 4in). Spread, 6m (20ft). Deciduous, hardy; well-drained – damp.

Sorbus aucuparia (rowan)

The rowan has divided leaves, which produce a light feathery effect. Large cream flower heads are produced in late spring. The autumn colour is particularly good and the berries produced are a vivid scarlet and very popular with birds. Height, 15m (49ft). Spread, 6m (20ft). Deciduous, hardy; well-drained – damp.

Taxodium distichum (swamp cypress)

This conifer enjoys moist conditions and will produce knee-like growths when planted by water. The light feathery foliage is lost in the autumn in a display of strong colour and the bark is an attractive red-brown. This is really only suitable for large spaces and gardens. Height, 30m (100ft). Spread, 10m (33ft). Deciduous, hardy; wet.

SHRUBS AND GRASSES

This group of plant material is appropriate to almost any site or size of garden. In contrast to trees, however, where one or two specimens can make a great impact, in general there is a need to plant in groups. Individual or isolated specimens can look lost or insignificant even in smaller gardens. Use the information given on the eventual spread of the plants as a guide for spacings but remember that plants are not static elements.

Spacing plant material with the mature spread in mind will lead to high initial maintenance as there will be strong competition from weeds. A mulch will help in this respect but the garden will still have an empty, immature appearance for some years. Many gardeners choose to plant at reduced distances for an earlier impact. This leads to restricted competition from weeds, but a higher long-term maintenance requirement when thinning or pruning becomes necessary.

Plant in odd-numbered groups for best effect using only carefully chosen plant material for specimen or accent use. The following list is made up of plants chosen particularly for their form in association with water. The grasses in particular come into their own in such circumstances for their textural value.

Acer palmatum 'Bloodgood' (Japanese maple)

There are many decorative Japanese maples from which to choose but this has a strong purple-red leaf and excellent autumn colour. The fine leaves produce a mound of texture. Height, 3m (10ft). Spread, 3m (10ft). Deciduous, hardy; well-drained.

The surrounding planting all but engulfs this reflective pool in a feast of colour and texture. The hard edges of the far side of the pool contrast well with the jungle of grasses and reeds.

Carex pendula (pendulous sedge)

This is a most graceful grass with arching stems and long, pendulous greenish-brown flower spikes produced in the summer. Height, 1m (3ft 3in). Spread, 1m (3ft 3in). Evergreen, hardy; well-drained–wet.

Ceratostigma plumbaginoides (hardy plumbago)

The flowers of Ceratostigma provide a mass of intense blue late in the year, useful for strong reflections. Height, 45cm (1ft 6in). Spread, 30cm (1ft). Deciduous, hardy; well-drained.

Cornus alba 'Sibirica' (dogwood)

The stems of this dogwood produce a display of fiery scarlet in the winter and this may be maintained by cutting the stems back in the spring to encourage new growth. The leaves also colour well. C. alba 'Kesselringii' has black stems. Height, 4m (13ft). Spread, 2m (6ft 6in). Deciduous, hardy; well-drained.

Cotinus coggygria (smoke tree)

The flower stems of Cotinus are smoke-like plumes produced in the summer but remaining on the plant into the autumn. This effect is coupled with brilliant autumn foliage colour. Height, 5m (16ft). Spread, 5m (16ft). Deciduous, hardy; well-drained.

Cotoneaster salicifolius

This is a particularly elegant form of cotoneaster with graceful spreading branches and long, willow-shaped leaves. The white flowers of spring are followed by clusters of red berries. Height 5m (16ft). Spread, 5m (16ft). Evergreen, hardy; well-drained – damp.

Euphorbia characias subsp. wulfenii

This textured Euphorbia produces large, yellow-green flowers, which contrast well with the blue-green foliage. Height, 1m (3ft 3in). Spread, 1.2m (4ft). Evergreen with biennial stems, hardy; moist but well-drained.

Fatsia japonica

The large, dark green leaves of this shrub provide an architectural structure and a good backdrop to poolside planting or a strong contrast to the smoothness of still water. White globular flower heads are produced in the autumn. Height, 3m (10ft). Spread, 3m (10ft). Evergreen; well-drained. Frost hardy, but may need protection from winds.

Hordeum jubatum (foxtail barley)

The main feature of this grass is the flower spike which appears in late summer as an arching silky plume. Unfortunately, the grass is relatively short-lived and usually treated as an annual. Height, 60cm (2ft). Spread, 30cm (1ft). Herbaceous, hardy; well-drained.

Juniperus × media 'Pfitzeriana'

The elegant structure of this Juniper produces horizontal, wide-spreading branches carrying grey-green foliage which could be used effectively to overhang water, or to disguise edges. J. × media 'Pfitzeriana Aurea' has golden foliage whilst J. × media 'Pfitzeriana Glauca' has blue-green leaves. Height, 3m (10ft). Spread, 5m (16ft). Evergreen, hardy; well-drained.

Miscanthus sinensis 'Gracillimus'

In contrast, this is one of the most architectural grasses with long arching leaves and tall flowering panicles produced in the autumn. Height, 1.5m (5ft). Spread, 1m (3ft 3in). Herbaceous, frost hardy; well-drained.

Nandina domestica (sacred bamboo)

The long dark green leaves of Nandina are reminiscent of bamboo and will colour purple when young or in the winter. Panicles of white flowers may be followed in autumn by red berries, particularly in warmer areas. Height, 2m (6ft 6in). Spread, 2m (6ft 6in). Evergreen, frost hardy; well-drained – damp.

Phormium tenax (New Zealand flax)

This architectural plant is mainly grown for its tall, sword-shaped, dark green leaves but, in addition, the flower spike reaches a height of 2.5–3m (8–10ft). Useful as a specimen or highlight. Height, 3m (10ft). Spread, 2m (6ft 6in). Evergreen, frost hardy; moist but well-drained.

Pseudosasa japonica (arrow bamboo)

This is one of the more common bamboos for garden cultivation but the erect and elegant stems are perfect for vertical emphasis alongside water. It is invasive and vigorous and should be introduced only after careful thought. Height, 5m (16ft). Spread, indefinite. Evergreen, hardy; damp – moist. Other bamboos such as *Phillostachys nigra, Sinarundinaria nitida* and the ground covering *Sasa veitchii* are also appropriate.

Rosa moyesii 'Geranium'

The brilliant red flowers of this species rose are carried on spreading, arching stems in summer. They are followed in the autumn by large red hips. Height, 3m (10ft). Spread, 3m (10ft). Deciduous, hardy; moist but well-drained.

Rubus cockburnianus

This ornamental bramble forms a graceful shrub with arching blue-white branches clothed with dark green fern-like leaves. Height, 3m (10ft). Spread, 3m (10ft). Deciduous, hardy; well-drained. Also of interest are *R.* 'Benenden', *R. thibetanus* and *R. tricolor*. The latter produces dense groundcover.

Spiraea 'Arguta' (bridal wreath)

In the spring, the branches of this Spirea are crammed with foaming sprays of cream-white flower to spectacular effect. Height, 2.5m (8ft). Spread, 2.5m (8ft). Deciduous, hardy; well-drained – damp.

Stipa gigantea (golden oat)

This elegant, tall grass produces a haze of delicate flower panicles of silver and gold which stay on the stems into the winter months. Height, 2.5m (8ft). Spread, 1m (3ft 3in). Evergreen, frost hardy; well-drained.

Viburnum plicatum 'Mariesii'

The cream flowers of this Viburnum, produced in late spring, are carried on tiers of horizontal branches for architectural effect. Height, 3m (10ft). Spread, 4m (13ft). Deciduous, hardy; well-drained – damp. Also of interest, *V.* × *bodnantense* 'Dawn', *V. rhytidophyllum* and *V. tinus*.

Yucca gloriosa (Adam's needle)

This is a dramatic, architectural shrub with spiky blue-green leaves and tall panicles of cream, bell-shaped flowers. Height, 2m (6ft 6in). Spread, 2m (6ft 6in). Evergreen, hardy; well-drained.

HERBACEOUS PLANTS

Herbaceous plants offer some of the most dramatic impact on the garden, particularly in association with water. Texture, shape and form are all important and the exuberance of summer growth is dynamic and exciting. Spacing can be difficult as they are almost always insignificant when purchased. Research overall heights and spreads and bear in mind that these dimensions are attainable over a much shorter time scale than with trees or shrubs. For this reason, they may be used as filler plants in the early, immature years of a garden.

Achillea filipendulina 'Gold Plate'

The flowers of this hardy perennial are flat plates of golden yellow providing good horizontal contrast and strong reflective colour in summer. Height, 1.2m (4ft). Spread, 60cm (2ft). Well-drained.

Alchemilla mollis (lady's mantle)

The soft felted leaves and sprays of yellow-green flowers produce a soft but intensely colourful display for the summer months. Ideal for edging or mass planting. Height, 50cm (20in). Spread, 50cm (20in). Well-drained – moist. Hardy.

Astilbe

The association of Astilbe with water is popular. They prefer moist soils and their strong, colourful blooms work well in reflections. Many forms are available, chosen mainly for colour. Height, about 60cm (2ft). Spread, up to 1m (3ft 3in). Moist.

Crambe cordifolia

This is a plant of contrasts which work well with water. The large, dark green leaves provide a textured base from which a cloud of tiny white flowers emerge as if floating in the air. Height, 2m (6ft 6in). Spread, 1.2m (4ft). Well-drained. Hardy.

Digitalis purpurea (foxglove)

The tall flowering spikes of foxglove, produced in summer, are a must for waterside locations and particularly for woodland water settings. D. *Purpurea* 'Alba' is a pure white form. Height, 1.5m (5ft). Spread, 60cm (2ft). Moist, but well-drained. Grown as a biennial; hardy.

Echinops ritro 'Veitch's Blue'

This decorative thistle produces dark-textured foliage and large purple-blue globular flowers on silver stems in late summer. Height, 1.2m (4ft). Spread, 1m (3ft 3in). Well-drained. Hardy.

Gunnera manicata

This must be the most spectacular of waterside plants. The leaves reach 1.5m (5ft) across and surround a huge pale green flowering spike, produced in early summer. The leaves die back in the winter and need to be protected from frost. Plant only after serious consideration as space is obviously of some concern. However, the bold foliage can be effective in smaller spaces for a heightened sense of drama. Height, 2.5m (8ft). Spread, 3m (10ft) minimum. Moist. Frost hardy, but requires wind protection.

Helleborus orientalis

These delicate winter-flowering plants produce ethereal blooms in haunting shades of burgundy, cream and pink, above dense, divided foliage. They relate well to still, reflective water. Height, 45cm (1ft 6in). Spread, 45cm (1ft 6in). Damp but well-drained soil. Hardy.

Hemerocallis (day lily)

The erect, iris-like foliage of the day lily contrasts well with a waterside setting and with large foliage speciess. Lily-like flowers in a wide range of colours are carried in the early summer, each lasting a day. Height, 1m (3ft 3in). Spread, 75cm (2ft 6in). Moist. Hardy.

The bold foliage and flower spikes of Rodgersia provide a perfect foil to water. Here the architectural effect is softened by the frothy flowers of Alchemilla.

Hosta (funkia, plantain lily)

The large, fleshy leaves of Hosta are ideal when seen against water. The leaf colours and variegations are myriad but all produce arching flower stems and delicate bell-shaped flowers in mid summer. Height, up to 1m (3ft 3in). Spread, 1m (3ft 3in). Moist but well-drained. Hardy. Many forms are available, mainly chosen for leaf quality.

Iris

One of the most common, yet also most beautiful, waterside plant, combining long sword-shaped leaves with exotic flowers in a wide range of colours and patterns. Many forms are available, mainly chosen for flower colour. Not all iris enjoy moist conditions and detailed planting requirements should be checked prior to purchase or planting. Height, up to 1.2m (4ft). Spread, often indefinite. Hardy.

Kniphofia (red-hot poker, torch lily)

An architectural perennial with sword-shaped leaves and dramatic flower spikes in shades of red, orange and yellow. The erect flowering stems and bright colours work well with water of any sort. Many forms are available, mainly chosen for flower colour. Height, 1m (3ft 3in). Spread, 1m (3ft 3in). Hardy.

Ligularia dentata 'Desdemona'

This is a dramatic plant with large black-green leaves tinted purple-red beneath. The flower stems are similarly dark but carry vivid warm yellow flowers from mid to late summer. Height, 1.2m (4ft). Spread, 1m (3ft 3in). Moist but well-drained. Hardy. L. *przewalskii* is also worth considering.

Ophiopogon planiscapus 'Nigrescens'

This spreading perennial produces black, grass-like foliage to dramatic effect. Works well with gravel or cobbles as a low groundcover. Height, 30cm (1ft). Spread, 30cm (1ft). Well-drained. Hardy.

Petasites japonicus var. giganteus

This is a vigorous grower and needs careful siting. The flowers are carried in early spring before the large fleshy leaves develop for which they are mainly cultivated. Height, 1m (3ft 3in). Spread, 2m (6ft 6in). Moist but well-drained. Hardy.

Polygonatum × hybridum (Solomon's seal)

The arching stems, delicate white bell-like pendent flowers and oval leaves make this an elegant addition to the water side. Height, 1.2m (4ft). Spread, 1m (3ft 3in). Well-drained. Hardy.

Primula

There are Primulas for almost every type of garden but many are suitable for water gardens either by association or by preference. They vary from low ground-covering species to the elegant and decorative candelabra primulas. Individual preferences should be checked prior to purchase or planting. Many forms are available, mainly chosen for their flower colour and form. Height, range from 15cm–1m (6in–3ft 3in). Spread, 15–30cm (6in–3ft 3in). Tender to hardy.

Rheum palmatum (ornamental rhubarb)

A magnificent foliage plant which grows dramatically over the summer – so fast that it is often said that one can sit and watch it grow. The texture and leaf form are of particular interest and value but the feathery, creamy-white flowers, produced in early summer, reach up to the sky. Rheum palmatum 'Arosanguineum' has red flowers. Height, 3m (10ft). Spread, 2m (6ft 6in). Well-drained. Hardy.

The delicate but colourful flowers of the candelabra primula produce stunning displays often associated with water or woodland gardens. Use them in drifts or with grasses and ferns.

Rodgersia podophylla

This is a perfect waterside plant with architectural foliage and tall cream stems of flower, produced in summer. The leaves have a bronze cast when young and are deeply veined. Height, 1m (3ft 3in). Spread, 60cm (2ft). Moist. Hardy.

Sisyrinchium striatum

The iris-like grey-green foliage is decorated with lemon-yellow flowers on erect stems in summer. Height, 60cm (2ft). Spread, 30cm (1ft). Well-drained – damp. Hardy.

FERNS AND GROUNDCOVER

Groundcover is essential in the contemporary garden. The decorative qualities of these plants are of great value, but it is their labour-saving aspect that is so important. By covering the ground with a carpet of foliage, they will supress weed growth and reduce maintenance considerably.

It is important to plant relatively densely in order to encourage competitive growth, although this can also lead to competition for specimen plants.

Ferns are splendid in association with water, their delicate tracery providing good textures and patterns. They particularly favour semi-shade and thus work well in woodland settings.

Bergenia stracheyi

The broad leathery leaves of this plant are the main decorative feature. It is best used as an edging or for mass ground cover. The pink flowers, produced in summer, can be a little vibrant but B. 'Silberlicht' gives a pale white-pink. Height, 30cm (1ft). Spread, 60cm (2ft). Evergreen, hardy; well-drained.

Dryopteris filix-mas (male fern)

The textured, mid-green leaves of this fern are strong and architectural. It prefers shady conditions. Height, 1.2m (4ft). Spread, 1m (3ft 3in). Deciduous, hardy; moist.

Geranium 'Johnson's Blue' (crane's bill geranium)

The deep purple-blue flowers of this hardy crane's bill, produced throughout summer, are set into mounds of dark-green textured foliage. Height, 30cm (1ft). Spread, 60cm (2ft). Herbaceous. Well-drained – damp. Many other forms of Geranium are suitable for inclusion in the water garden though they do not enjoy really wet conditions. Tolerant of shade.

Hedera colchica (Persian ivy)

The leaves of this ivy are large and black-green, producing a dramatic carpet of foliage when used as a groundcover. Height as groundcover, 30cm (1ft). Spread, 5–10m (2–4in). Evergreen, hardy; well-drained.

Helxine soleirolii syn. Soleirolia soleirolii (baby's tears)

This plant produces tiny bright green leaves, ideal for cracks between paving or to soften the edges of pools. Hardy, but in colder areas it may not survive frost. Height, 5cm (2in). Spread, indefinite. Evergreen; moist.

Matteuccia struthiopteris (ostrich plume fern)

The leaves of this fern are reminiscent of a shuttlecock, with light green sterile fronds protecting dark-brown fertile fronds. Height, 1m (3ft 3in). Spread, 60cm (2ft). Deciduous, hardy; wet.

Osmunda regalis (royal fern)

This regal fern lives up to its name, producing tall, elegant, bright-green fronds. When mature, it produces tall red-brown flower spikes. Height, 2m (6ft 6in). Spread, 1m (3ft 3in). Deciduous, hardy; wet.

Polygonum bistorta 'Superbum'

An excellent, low groundcovering plant with pale pink flower heads, produced in early to late summer, held high above bright green foliage. Prefers moist conditions. Height, 75cm (2ft 6in). Spread, 60cm (2ft). Herbaceous, hardy; damp.

Polystichum setiferum (soft shield fern)

The divided leaves of this fern provide an excellent foil to still, reflective water. Height, 60cm (2ft). Spread, 45cm (18in). Evergreen or semi-evergreen, hardy; moist but well-drained.

123

Trollius europaeus

These bright-flowering groundcover plants enjoy pool or stream side locations. The tightly cupped flowers, carried in spring, are the main attraction. The leaves are mid-green and deeply divided. Height, 60cm (2ft). Spread, 45cm (1ft 6in). Herbaceous, hardy; moist – wet.

BULBS

Bulbs offer some of the most decorative flowers and will often perform on a seasonal basis at some of the most difficult times of the year. The larger species should be used in a similar way to specimen shrubs, planted in groups for spectacular effect. The smaller species are more suitable for wide, spreading drifts, providing expansive sheets of colour and pattern.

Allium christophii

The larger globular heads of purple-pink flowers, carried in summer, are excellent when seen emerging form low groundcover. They will work well as reflected shapes. Height, 45cm (1ft 6in). Spread, 20cm (8in). Well-drained. Frost hardy.

Cardiocrinum giganteum (giant lily)

Tall, fragrant cream flowers are carried high in the air in summer for dramatic effect. The shiny dark green leaves are large at the base of the plant and become smaller towards the top of the stems. Height, 3m (10ft). Spread, 1m (3ft 3in). Moist. Frost hardy.

Crocosmia 'Lucifer'

The fiery red flowers of this plant produced in mid summer, are true to its name. The iris-like leaves provide good vertical emphasis in planting associations. Height, 1m (3ft 3in). Spread, 60cm (2ft). Well-drained. Frost hardy.

Cyclamen coum subsp. coum 'Album'

This winter-flowering Cyclamen produces low patterned leaves decorated with white butterfly-like flowers. C. hederifolium and C. repandum may also prove of interest. Height, 15cm (6in). Spread, 20cm (8in). Well-drained. Frost hardy.

Fritillaria imperialis (crown imperial)

This stately plant carries a crown of orange-yellow bell-shaped drooping flowers amid pale green leaves in the spring. F. imperialis 'Maxima Lutea' is a yellow form. Height, 1.5m (5ft). Spread, 30cm (1ft). Well-drained. Hardy.

Fritillaria pallidiflora

In contrast to the above, this fritillary hides its light, green-yellow flowers which are produced in spring. It has grey-green foliage. Height, 60cm (2ft). Spread, 15cm (6in). Well-drained. Hardy.

Galanthus nivalis 'Flore Pleno' (snowdrop)

These excellent but often overlooked bulbs provide a dazzling winter display if mass planted. The flowers are white and the leaves grey-green. Height, 10cm (4in). Spread, 10cm (4in). Damp. Hardy.

Lilium regale (regal lily)

One of the most beautiful and intensely fragrant lilies with pure white trumpet flowers, produced in summer. Height, up to 2m (6ft 6in). Spread, 15cm (6in). Well-drained. Hardy.

Nerine bowdenii

This is an autumn-flowering bulb producing decorative and intricate pink flowers on a stout stem. Height, 60cm (2ft). Spread, 15cm (6in). Well-drained. Frost hardy.

Appendix

MAINTENANCE

The maintenance of water features once created and established is essential to their future success. As with any garden. there is always a temptation to sit back and relax, and, of course, this is what any garden is for, but the assumption that borders will look after themselves is dangerous. Similarly, with water features, there is a need for regular maintenance to keep abreast of competitive plant growth or simply to prevent deterioration and future problems.

The requirements fall easily into seasonal categories and the major tasks are outlined below.

Spring

Divide and transplant all existing aquatic and bog plants. This can be a major task but needs to be carried out only about once every three years.

Plant new aquatic and bog plants.

Check for winter damage to rigid pool structures or to poorer quality flexible liners, such as PVC. Remove any rotting vegetation and clean out rigid or lined water features if necessary.

Remove any pumping and electrical equipment left in position over winter. Clean and check these fittings, ensuring that all insulation is still intact and that the pumps run free. (Pumps should be overhauled regularly by a specialist.)

Increase the flow rate of filtration tanks and beds, checking that all filtration equipment is operating correctly.

If a pond is to be drained completely, it is best to drain the water level down by two-thirds. This will allow easier and safer access, and it is also easier to remove fish with a reduced water level. Remove all wildlife (or as much as possible) to a holding tank, which should be filled with the water drained from the pond. The plants can then be lifted and the remaining water drained. The debris and silt should be taken out using soft edge dustpans or, on larger areas, plastic shovels.

For larger pools and lakes, dredging can be carried out, taking care to preserve existing wildlife and aquatic vegetation where possible. These operations are best carried out by specialist companies.

Summer

Continually remove all dead leaves and old flower heads from plants to reduce the amount of debris in the water.

Watch for signs of aphid attack. Treat with caution if discovered, because aquatic plants are more easily damaged by over spraying, and unless the plants to be treated are within a confined area of water, you will need to seek specialist help. In the UK the National Rivers Authority will have to be consulted and permission obtained before treatment can be carried out.

Planting new aquatics is best in early to midsummer, allowing time for the plant material to become established before the onset of winter. Existing plants, especially lilies, can still be divided. Old plants are best discarded in favour of the young plants, which will produce better flowers. Apply slow-release sachets once a year to all lilies and aquatics.

Ponds can be cleaned out throughout the summer, although the risk of disturbing wildlife and the growing aquatics is much greater than in the spring.

Regularly clean pump filters, jets and strainers.

Algae may be a problem, especially during periods of high temperature. Treat if required but again permission will be necessary if your water feature is not confined.

Water evaporation will be at its worst over the summer, particularly if you run a fountain or a waterfall. If a hose ban is not in effect, aim to keep the water level constant at the desired level. The introduction of new water will help maintain water quality, especially if fish are involved.

Some liners will deteriorate if exposed to sunlight and when water levels drop edges are automatically exposed.

Autumn

Remove foliage as it dies back from all aquatic plants. Cut down stems and foliage to below the surface of the water.

Do not remove or interfere with floating plants as they depend on their buds falling from their dying foliage, which sinks to the bottom of the pool for over-wintering.

Remove all tender aquatics and place in temporary containers to be over-wintered under glass.

Prune trees, shrubs and bog plants growing in the vicinity of the water feature.

Winter

Complete all the removal of dead aquatic foliage.

Remove all pumps into storage, unless the system is to be operated throughout the year. Make sure that the pumps are thoroughly drained of all water prior to storage. Treat all exposed metal parts with a protective light oil.

It is possible to install heaters, which may be necessary if fish are present. They will also reduce or prevent damage to rigid pools caused by a build-up of ice, which can creat pressure against the pool sides. Alternatively, you can float a ball in the pool to prevent ice building up.

Useful Equipment

Fish nets of various sizes are useful for the removal of wildlife and also for the collection of debris and leaves from the water.

Sump or sludge pump Unlike most water pumps these will take comparatively larger solids, depending on the model employed. Gravel and other large particles will not generally cause damage. Pumps cannot be used without a high water content and in many cases water will need to be added to assist pumping operations.

Pressure washers are useful for cleaning flexible liners and rigid ponds. They are especially effective against algae.

Ladders or staging can be used to give access over smaller garden ponds. Scaffolding boards or similar timbers should not be used because they tend to bow under pressure.

A high-pressure vacuum such as those used for swimming pools may be used to keep rigid pools clear of leaves. They are unsuitable for ponds that include debris or silt as the system will easily clog.

Chest waders will allow direct access for pruning, clearance activity and general maintenance, but safety should be considered at all times. Always be aware of water depth. Chest waders are preferred to thigh waders or boots as a great deal of work is carried out in a crouching position, which would, therefore, enable water to enter shorter boots. Most waders are designed for fishing and will be fitted with studs for improved grip. They are not appropriate for artificial pool maintenance, as the studs may damage the liner; studless boots are preferred.

Pruning equipment may be used for the removal of foliage and root growth. However, all cutting implements should be used with extreme caution in pools with flexible liners. Often it is best to remove the plant material to be pruned or split to dry land to prevent accidental damage.

Specialist help should be sought for repairs to be carried out to any type of pool construction, including flexible liners. If in doubt over any maintenance activity, consult a specialist.

INDEX

Page numbers in *italics* refer to captions to illustrations